# PEOPLE OF THE PLAGUE

HORRORS OF HISTORY

# PEOPLE OF THE PLAGUE

## T. NEILL ANDERSON

ini Charlesbridge

Copyright © 2014 by MTM Publishing, Inc.
All rights reserved, including the right of reproduction in whole or in part
in any form. Charlesbridge and colophon are registered trademarks of
Charlesbridge Publishing, Inc.

MTM Publishing, Inc.
435 West 23rd Street, #8C
New York, NY 10011
www.mtmpublishing.com

President: Valerie Tomaselli
Series creator: Hilary Poole
Designer: Annemarie Redmond
Illustrator: Richard Garratt
Copyeditor: Josette Haddad
Academic advisor: James Higgins

Published by Charlesbridge
85 Main Street
Watertown, MA 02472
(617) 926-0329
www.charlesbridge.com

**Library of Congress Cataloging-in-Publication Data**
Anderson, T. Neill.
Horrors of history : people of the plague / by T. Neill Anderson.
p. cm
Summary: The destiny of Barium, Wilmer, Harriet, and other
Philadelphians is threatened when the most severe flu epidemic in U.S. history
fills hospitals—and cemeteries—to capacity in 1918.
ISBN 978-1-58089-518-7 (reinforced for library use)
ISBN 978-1-60734-542-8 (ebook)
ISBN 978-1-60734-641-8 (ebook pdf)
1. Influenza Epidemic, 1918–1919—Pennsylvania—Philadelphia—Fiction.
[1. Influenza Epidemic, 1918–1919—Fiction. 2. Philadelphia (Pa.)—
History—20th century—Fiction.] I. Title.
PZ7.A5516Hs 2014
[Fic]—dc23                                    2013033038

Printed in China
(hc) 10 9 8 7 6 5 4 3 2 1

Display type set in Cracked and text type set in Adobe Caslon Pro
Printed and bound February 2014
by Jade Productions in Heyuan, Guangdong, China

# Table of Contents

*Prologue   ix*

CHAPTER 1: Coughs and Sneezes Spread
           Diseases . . . . . . . . . . . . . . . . . 1

CHAPTER 2: Spitting Equals Death . . . . . . 17

CHAPTER 3: Spasms . . . . . . . . . . . . . . . . . 30

CHAPTER 4: The Sick Hall. . . . . . . . . . . . 43

CHAPTER 5: "Do You See the Angels?". . . . 53

CHAPTER 6: To the Deadhouse . . . . . . . . . 64

CHAPTER 7: Deeply Cyanotic. . . . . . . . . . . 77

CHAPTER 8: Vermin . . . . . . . . . . . . . . . . . 93

CHAPTER 9: An Uncanny Population. . . . 106

CHAPTER 10: Under the Dogwood Tree . . 120

*Epilogue   139*
*Author's Note   143*
*Photo Credits   146*

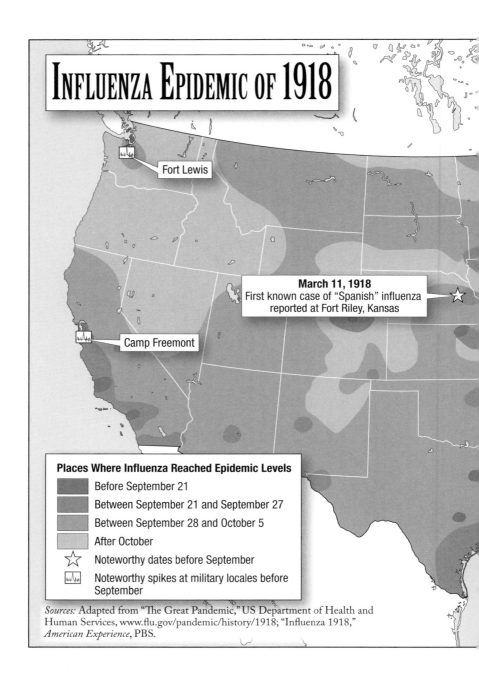

# INFLUENZA EPIDEMIC OF 1918

Fort Lewis

**March 11, 1918**
First known case of "Spanish" influenza
reported at Fort Riley, Kansas

Camp Freemont

**Places Where Influenza Reached Epidemic Levels**

Before September 21

Between September 21 and September 27

Between September 28 and October 5

After October

☆ Noteworthy dates before September

Noteworthy spikes at military locales before
September

*Sources:* Adapted from "The Great Pandemic," US Department of Health and
Human Services, www.flu.gov/pandemic/history/1918; "Influenza 1918,"
*American Experience*, PBS.

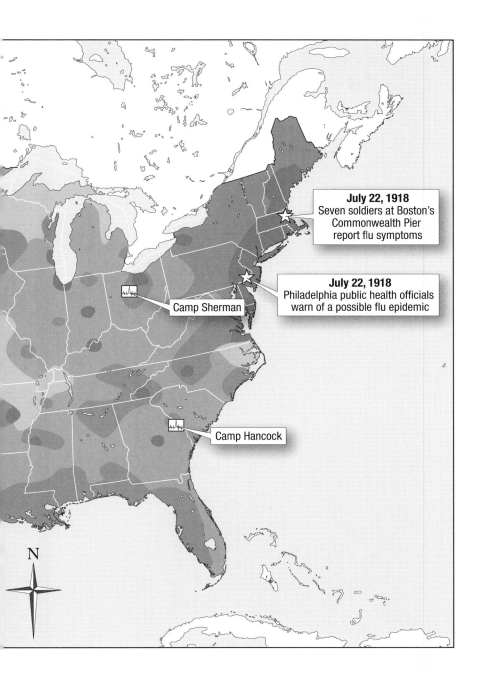

**July 22, 1918**
Seven soldiers at Boston's
Commonwealth Pier
report flu symptoms

**July 22, 1918**
Philadelphia public health officials
warn of a possible flu epidemic

Camp Sherman

Camp Hancock

N

*This was a flu that put people into bed as if they'd been hit with a two-by-four. That turned into pneumonia, that turned people blue and black and killed them. It was a flu out of some sort of a horror story.*

—Alfred Crosby, historian
("Influenza 1918." *American Experience.* PBS, 1988.)

# PROLOGUE

*September 17, 1918*

A YOUNG MAN DRESSED IN a white T-shirt and white, navy-issued trousers stumbled into the reception area of Pennsylvania Hospital. His wet face was the color of a bruise, and he struggled to hold himself upright. Two nurses put him in a wheelchair and rushed him through the swinging doors of the emergency ward.

"Another sailor from the Navy Yard, Doctor." The nurse glanced back out to reception and saw three other young men, also dressed in white, tumbling out of a navy ambulance. "And it looks like there are more coming."

The emergency ward was lined with small beds, most filled with sailors, all coughing, moaning, and chattering deliriously. Five doctors and fifteen nurses moved among them, checking temperatures, offering wet cloths, and pouring cups of water. With each passing minute, another empty bed in the large room was taken by a new patient. The navy hospital on the very south end of the city had run out of beds the day before, when almost one hundred soldiers all reported ill at the same time. Pennsylvania Hospital had become the destination for all new reported cases.

"This is bad, Betty," one nurse whispered to another. "It's one thing to have a bunch of sick men at the Navy Yard—now they're coming to a civilian hospital? God knows what those boys have been exposed to."

"But what can we do, Frances?" Betty asked. "We can't just turn them away."

Frances approached another bed. She pulled out a thermometer, then stopped, staring straight ahead and squinting.

"Frances?" Betty wiped some blood from under her patient's nose and looked over at her colleague. "Frances, what's wrong?"

Frances dropped the thermometer and it shattered. She wobbled for a moment and collapsed.

Betty rushed over, putting her hand on Frances's forehead. "Frances! Can you hear me?"

A long, low moan escaped Frances's mouth. Blood trickled out of her nose. Before Betty could react, another nurse collapsed and landed at her feet. A doctor in the next row of beds, bleeding through his medical mask, swayed slowly and fell over. A nurse nearby collapsed against the wall and slid down. Betty jumped up to run out to reception, but a doctor slammed into her and fainted, sending them both to the floor.

Betty wriggled out from under him and took off, screaming, into the hallway. A few steps from the reception desk she stumbled to a stop and slumped against the wall, wiping her nose: blood. Looking back into the emergency ward, she saw all the doctors and nurses writhing on the floor as dozens of patients begged for help. She slid down the wall and onto the hallway floor.

Influenza had come to Philadelphia.

# Coughs and Sneezes Spread Diseases

Two DIRT-SMEARED CHILDREN, A YOUNG boy and his older sister, marched side by side down South Philadelphia's grimy, trash-strewn South Street. They stomped along, swinging their arms in their best imitation of American soldiers, and shouted out a familiar patriotic chant:

> *Tramp, tramp, tramp, the boys are marching.*
> *I spy Kaiser at the door.*
> *We'll get a lemon pie and we'll squash him in his eye*
> *And there won't be any Kaiser anymore.*

The two halted at Broad Street, already crowded with families and clusters of people, even at the early hour of 8:00 a.m. They turned around and marched back up South Street, still chanting in rhythm. When they reached their family's tenement, squeezed in among the other extremely narrow dwellings running along the entire block, they stopped.

"Who's Kaiser, anyway?" the boy, six-year-old Harry Milani, asked his twelve-year-old sister, Harriet.

"Kaiser's not his name, silly," Harriet said. "He's the bad man we're fighting in Germany. 'Kaiser' is what they call him, like we call Woodrow Wilson 'president.'"

Harriet grinned mischievously, then turned back to her brother. "You know what the kaiser does to little kids, don't you, Harry?" she asked, stepping toward him. Harry looked at her and shook his head.

"No," he said uneasily.

"You don't?" Harriet looked at him with mock surprise. "I can't believe Mommy never told you. Well, I don't want to scare you, but . . . legend has it that the kaiser comes at night to punish

The influenza epidemic occurred while Americans were concerned with World War I. A Philadelphia newspaper cartoon, circa 1917, expresses the idea that the United States (Lady Liberty) needed to rescue Europe (the damsel in distress) from Germany.

children for being naughty. He's the opposite of Santa Claus. And he's got a long mustache that he waxes with . . . *the blood of little American boys!*"

"No, he doesn't!" Harry insisted.

"Oh yes! Yes, he does!" Harriet moved in closer, her hands reaching out toward Harry's face. "And I hear he's looking for a few more boys named Harry!"

Harry giggled and screamed as his sister pinched his cheeks and mussed his brown hair. Squirming loose, he made a run for it but slammed right into an older boy walking by. The two stumbled on the sidewalk for a moment before regaining their footing. In the tussle the older boy dropped a white paper bag he'd been carrying.

"Harry!" Harriet shouted. She looked at the boy that Harry had bounded into. "Sorry, Barium."

"Sorry, Barium!" Harry repeated.

"It's okay," fifteen-year-old Barium Epp said, smiling and picking up his bag. "Barium" wasn't the name his parents had given him. That was "Barry." But he'd earned a new name the previous year when word got around that he'd failed his first chemistry test at high school, only getting one question right. The answer to that question was "barium." And now he'd never live it down.

"Whatcha got in the bag?" Harry asked.

"Harry! Don't be so nosy!" Harriet scolded.

"Oh, just some medicine for my mom. She's sick."

"Oh no," Harry gasped. "She can't go out and watch the parade?"

"Nah, she's in bed. Probably gonna stay there, for today at least." Barium looked over at his house, a few down from the

Milanis'. "She'll be able to hear it from her bedroom, though. I'll try to come out for a spell."

"I was just telling Harry all about the kaiser," Harriet said, winking.

"What about him?"

"Oh, you know . . . how he hides under bad children's beds at night . . ."

Harry looked with keen interest at Barium to see what he'd say. Barium returned the look and grinned.

"You believe that, Harry?" he asked. Harry slowly and uncertainly shook his head.

"Yeah, neither do I," Barium agreed. "I've never seen the kaiser, and I'm *always* in trouble."

"Barium!" Harriet shouted. "Don't ruin it!"

"Sorry. Boys have to look out for each other—right, Harry? Gotta go get this medicine to my mom. Maybe see you at the parade?" He tipped his cap and strode to his family's house.

"Harriet," Harry said, watching Barium go, "why wouldn't the kaiser just hide in the closet?"

---

Dr. Wilmer Krusen, director of the Philadelphia Department of Public Health and Charities, was tired. He stood in the main building of the Holmesburg Poorhouse, which was being converted into an emergency hospital. It would be fitted with four hundred beds and staffed with nurses and doctors, many from outside the city.

It hadn't been easy. Five days ago he'd designated influenza a reportable illness for the first time in Philadelphia's history and begun broadcasting pleas for doctors and nurses and for available buildings that could be used as hospitals. The city's regular hospitals were already filled up with influenza patients, and he had a sickening feeling that there would be many more to come. For two weeks he'd been hearing frightening reports from Boston about shocking jumps in the number of influenza cases there. It was looking more and more like this pestilence would envelop his own city.

The phone rang.

"Krusen," he said. "Yes. I'm afraid the parade is still on, yes. . . . It's no use, the mayor refuses to cancel. . . . Yes, and we'll be ready to take patients today. . . . Okay." Wilmer held the phone receiver away from his ear and waited for the man on the other end to stop yelling.

"I know, Doctor. I know. I'm well aware of the implications. . . . I've done all I can, believe me. . . . The parade will go on, there's nothing to be done. We've just got to fight this thing the best way we can now."

He hung up.

It had been one of the physicians over at Blockley Hospital, flabbergasted that Wilmer had not canceled the parade. "As if I even had the power," Wilmer said to himself.

Wilmer sighed and, under his breath, muttered what he wished he could have said on the phone: "Yes, I'm a doctor, but I answer to a damned politician."

Wilmer hadn't had a decent night's sleep in many days. Ever since the first flu cases had started cropping up among sailors and soldiers in the Navy Yard, his life had been overtaken. He'd hoped that a quarantine would keep the illness confined. When sick soldiers and sailors began to die—fourteen deaths the first week, twenty-nine deaths so far this week—the army and navy converted the United Service Club on Walnut Street into an emergency hospital. All sick workers were to report there at the first sign of flu-like symptoms in order to halt the spread of the disease. But it continued infecting more, ripping through the Navy Yard with alarming speed. Philadelphia's civilian population would be next.

Wilmer certainly understood the mayor wanting the parade to go on as planned—parades were popular, and politicians wanted to be popular. But Wilmer was a public health official, and popularity wasn't part of his job description. If he'd had the power, he would have set up quarantine stations and enforced a curfew. But quarantines weren't popular, with the public or with politicians. Particularly the politician who had the power to fire him. And besides, the quarantine at the Navy Yard had failed utterly to halt the spread of the illness.

Instead, Wilmer had ordered the distribution of twenty thousand posters that warned of the presence of influenza in the city and cautioned Philadelphians about the dangers of coughing and sneezing in public. These posters had gone up all over the city. And to what effect? Just this week the health board had recorded its eleven hundredth flu case. The health warnings were all being drowned out by an altogether different public relations campaign.

"This damn parade," he muttered. "All for this damn war."

After four years on the sidelines, America had finally gotten involved in the Great War in Europe. That hadn't surprised Wilmer so much—he'd always suspected that President Wilson wouldn't be able to live up to his reelection promise to keep the country out of the war. What *had* surprised him was the enthusiasm with which his fellow citizens got behind the decision. Once the country committed its citizens and industry to the war

A Seattle streetcar conductor refuses to let a passenger board without a face mask. Likewise, in Philadelphia, Wilmer Krusen recognized how public places were dangerous incubators of influenza.

effort, an impassioned patriotism gripped the nation. *And here we are today,* Wilmer thought. A fourth Liberty Loan Parade to sell war bonds. Too many doctors and nurses away in Europe when they were needed here. All of Philadelphia abuzz with patriotic fervor, converging on Broad Street downtown in just a few hours. Marching arm in arm. Breathing on each other, touching, hugging, kissing, sharing mugs of beer or soda . . . and who knows what else. Wilmer shuddered.

He'd wanted to cancel the Liberty Loan Parade. Indeed, several private doctors had begged him to call it off, including the doctor at Blockley with whom he'd just spoken. If only he had the power. Yes, in theory, as the health director, he made decisions about public health risks, which this parade clearly was. But his was an appointed position; he served at the plea-sure—and the whim—of the mayor. And Thomas B. Smith, the mayor of this, one of the country's largest and most important cities, wasn't about to cancel a parade: Philadelphians' determi-nation to win the war and their passionate support for their boys in uniform would be on display for the entire nation! Mayor Smith was already getting bad press in the *Philadelphia Inquirer* for his city management style, which the paper called "corrupt." The newspapers would be calling for his head if he canceled a war-funding drive that would be the most spectacular parade in Philadelphia's history. Wilmer had tried to reason with Mayor Smith and convince him that the parade put the citizens of Philadelphia in danger. But to no avail.

"*Shoganai,*" Wilmer said to himself, recalling a Japanese expression he had heard once and had always liked for its calm simplicity: "It can't be helped." This peculiar strain of influenza was a monster that no medical treatment could yet slay. The only weapons at their disposal were lamentably weak in the face of such a ferocious opponent. Sure, there was aspirin, the relatively new wonder drug, which could reduce fever, pain, and inflammation. There was morphine for a bad cough and body pains. Caffeine and digitalis for heart stimulation. And, of course, there were all sorts of experimental home treatments that he knew didn't do much good beyond allowing people to feel as though they were doing something to help: camphor bags hung around the neck, Vicks chest and back rubs, whiskey and brandy concoctions. But there was no cure. All he could do was try to work within the constraints he found himself in. That's why he was setting up this emergency hospital. That's why there were plans for more.

After this parade they would certainly need them.

---

Thomas Ryan, age eighteen, marveled at the size of the crowd.

"Can you believe this?" he asked his nineteen-year-old friend Tim. They were squeezed up against a telephone pole plastered all over with Liberty Loan Parade posters.

"For Home and Country," one poster declared, showing a soldier hugging his wife and little daughter.

"Fight or Buy Bonds," insisted another, depicting a beautiful woman draped in a white gown and holding an American flag triumphantly above her head.

Beside Tim's head, also pasted to the pole among the parade flyers, was another: "Cover Your Mouth! Influenza Is Spread by Droplets Sprayed from Nose and Throat."

"It's surely larger than the last one," Tim said.

The parade was in full swing. The young men stepped carefully through the crowd, weaving between people and ducking to avoid swinging banners and waving arms. They finally came to a saloon on Broad Street, where they leaned against the large front windows.

Both sides of Broad Street heaved with people craning their necks to get the best view of the parade route. Church bells clanged, clashing with trolley bells that heralded the arrival of even more spectators. Police whistles mixed with the chatter of thousands of people and with the drum rolls and the burping of trombones, trumpets, and tubas coming from the army marching band now visible on the street.

A full twenty-three blocks of Broad Street were blocked off for the Liberty Loan Parade, all the way from Diamond Street to Mifflin Street. Each and every block was filled with marchers, and each and every marcher was being raucously celebrated by the throngs of Philadelphians. All two hundred thousand people in attendance, many waving American flags and banners, wore their patriotic best—red, white, and blue skirts, shirts, sweaters, jackets, hats. Mothers hugged their children, fathers kissed their wives and held sons and daughters on their shoulders, siblings pushed each other and laughed, giddy friends linked arms and swayed back and forth as line after line of marchers—firemen, policemen, school groups, labor unions, marching bands, infantrymen—glided past.

An excited roar soared through the crowd as formations of military aircraft flew overhead, followed by puffs of smoke discharged from anti-aircraft guns placed up and down Broad Street.

"Wow, I'm glad we came into town for this," Tim said, looking at the vapor trails in the sky, "but I'm starting to wonder when we'll be able to get back to Saint Charles."

The two young men had departed from Saint Charles Borromeo Seminary, in nearby Lower Merion Township, early that morning in order to have a full day away. Both had been craving a taste of the hustle and bustle of Philadelphia, which they rarely had a chance to visit, and the Liberty Loan Parade

A 1918 public-health poster from Philadelphia shows a demon arising from a pool of saliva.

was a perfect excuse to escape into the city. Their Saturdays were usually quiet and contemplative—full of study, Bible reading, Mass, prayer, and the various menial jobs they did to maintain the sanctuary and the pristine campus.

"Don't spoil it, Tim!" Thomas laughed, elbowing his friend in the side. "I've never even seen a real live plane before! We'll get back to confess our misdeeds soon enough. But first we gotta actually do at least one misdeed!"

Tim smiled. "Yeah, okay. I guess we should make it a proper day off. Hey, is that Leo?" Tim pointed to a man sitting by himself at a table inside the saloon, his back to them.

"I think it is," Thomas said. "I thought he'd be practicing his scales today."

"Looks like he left his cello back in his room." Tim grinned, pointing at the pint of beer in Leo's hand. "And he brought Richard with him." Another young man sat down next to Leo, pointed his finger at the far wall, and took a secret sip of Leo's beer as Leo looked away.

"Shall we join them?" Thomas asked, not waiting for an answer before opening the saloon door and hurrying in.

Tim shrugged, following Thomas inside. As the door closed behind him, the September wind blew a flyer off a nearby telephone pole. It fluttered toward the saloon, landing faceup on the sidewalk in front of the door.

It read: "Coughs and Sneezes Spread Diseases."

———•◦•———

Harry and Harriet jostled among the other parade-goers, squeezing through to the front of the crowd on Broad Street at the corner of Fitzwater. Before them marched a block of firemen, followed by a group of schoolchildren waving banners of their school colors. Then along rolled a tank pulling a large cannon, sending excited oohs and aahs of approval rippling through the crowd.

"Hey, kids! Harry! Harriet!" Mrs. Milani called from behind a clog of spectators on the sidewalk. "Don't get too close to the road!" She looked over at her husband with worry. "*Mio dio,* they'll get trampled."

"They'll be fine. Let them have their fun." Mr. Milani made eye contact with Harry as the boy looked back, excitedly pointing to the cannon. Mr. Milani smiled, took off his cap, and waved it in the air.

"Nothing like a parade to bring the entire city outside to clap and scream for a bunch of people walking in the middle of the street," Mrs. Milani said. Soon the sounds of a marching band emerged through the cacophony of the crowd. "At least some of them can play instruments."

"And drive tanks." Mr. Milani laughed as another tank rolled up behind the band. It stopped close to the children in the front of the crowd and turned around and around in several circles as the crowd squealed its appreciation. The tank stopped after a few revolutions, then turned to circle the other way around, to even more applause.

Harry hopped excitedly in place, clapping his hands together as the tank performed its tricks. Behind the tank came a truck pulling an unexpected—and very large—piece of cargo: an elephant. Harry shrieked with glee at the giant animal and watched it raptly as it glided past. A few more tanks and army trucks and cannons rolled by, followed by another few regiments of soldiers, and then finally the last marchers in the parade appeared—a group of elementary-school students, flanked by a few of their teachers, all holding signs saying "Show Your Button." The crowd roared, and many people held up the victory buttons they'd purchased at the parade, waving them in the air.

"Look!" Harriet shouted, pointing diagonally across the street, where one of the large cannons was now perched in the middle of Lombard Street. People were scurrying up, touching it, and taking pictures.

"I wanna see it closer!" Harry said.

"Better ask Mommy and Daddy," Harriet warned. Harry turned and squeezed through the crowd, looking all around for his parents.

"Harry!" Mr. Milani yelled from behind a crowd of people. "Harry, where's your sister?" Harry turned around guiltily, realizing he'd just up and left her behind in his haste.

"Right here, Daddy!" Harriet shouted, emerging from a throng of spectators. "Harry wants to go see the cannon in the street over there."

"Let's all go," Mrs. Milani said, taking her husband's hand. "Best if we stick together."

The Milani family wove their way through the crowd and joined the people admiring the cannon on Lombard Street. Mr. Milani lifted Harry up so the boy could touch the chase of the cannon.

"Wow . . ." Harry reached out and gingerly ran his hand along it, as if it would explode if he stroked it too hard. "It's cold, Daddy!"

"And you're heavy, my boy." His father laughed. "Gonna have to put you down. Let's give others a chance to see."

Crowds gather to watch the Liberty Loan Parade in downtown Philadelphia, September 18, 1918.

Mr. Milani deposited Harry on the ground and, sure enough, new groups of men, women, and children approached the cannon and ran their eager hands along the chase, the muzzle, the lip, and the wheels.

"Okay now," Mr. Milani said, looking at his children. "Who wants a hot dog?"

———•◦•———

Barium sat in a chair in his mother's bedroom, his eyes red and swollen with tears. He heard the jovial music of the marching band as well as the whoops and hollers of excited parade-goers outside. The happy sounds all around made the scene before him even more hideous.

He wiped some of his tears away and looked down at the bag he'd brought back from the pharmacy. He held it with an iron grip and couldn't bring himself to let go. He gazed up at his mother. She lay in bed, her eyes closed. Her face was dark yellow, and her nose was caked with dried blood. Her hands rested stiffly on her belly.

When he'd left to get the medicine, she was awake and softly singing along to the music she could hear the band playing one block over.

He'd only been away for twenty minutes. He wondered how long she'd been gone. And how she could possibly have died before he even got back.

# Spitting Equals Death

Wilmer Krusen couldn't remember the names of the men gathered in the mayor's office at city hall. He hadn't slept in days, and his brain was strained from managing Philadelphia's health workers, corralling volunteer doctors and nurses into emergency hospitals, meeting with morticians and coroners to discuss how to deal with the bodies that were starting to pile up in the streets, on porches, and outside funeral homes. He was far too tired to recall details like the names of these two men from Boston and New York.

He knew the mayor himself, of course. His boss, Thomas B. Smith. Mayor Smith lived his life as if he couldn't bear the thought of anyone forgetting his name. He had a nameplate on his office door and on his desk, and he had his name engraved on his pocket watch and on his money clip. He had even bestowed upon his son the only name that mattered: his own.

Mayor Smith usually monopolized meetings, impressing upon everyone the many demands on his time and the important people he'd be meeting later to discuss "business."

"I'm going to get so-and-so on the horn," he often said in his raspy voice, "and get this problem solved." These "so-and-so's" might be the high-and-mighty political party bosses who owed him a favor, or lowly tavern owners who were happy to help the mayor with anything he wanted so long as they could keep their liquor licenses.

Yes, Wilmer knew that the mayor could deal very well with many of Philadelphia's problems—legally or illegally. This was the man who'd recently been indicted for firing a reformer from the playground commission and replacing him with a more friendly Republican. But this . . . this was one problem that had left the mayor speechless. Instead, the out-of-towners—officials from Boston and New York, here about Philadelphia's response to an epidemic of historic proportions—were doing most of the talking.

"More than one thousand, as of yesterday," Boston said.

"One thousand dead," Wilmer repeated back. "And more cases every day, I presume."

"Countless," Boston replied. "We have over three hundred emergency hospitals staffed with whatever doctors and nurses have come forward to volunteer. But the number of patients is overwhelming our medics. You must continue to send out word for volunteers. Get the church involved."

New York nodded and stroked his white beard, a grimace on his lips. "But be careful of causing panic," he said. "New Yorkers are beside themselves. Doctors and nurses are scarce, and folks are getting desperate. We had a case yesterday of a nurse being kidnapped by a father whose children were deathly ill. . . ."

"All our hospitals are full, and there are lines out the door," Wilmer said. "Almost a hundred died yesterday."

A silence enveloped the room. A few moments later the mayor broke it.

"This is a damned invasion!" he said. "It was your boys from Boston that brought this thing into our Navy Yard!" Wilmer winced at this.

"It would have found its way here with or without 'our boys,'" Boston said coldly.

In New York City—a metropolis plagued almost as severely as Philadelphia—a mailman takes precautions against the flu.

"The whole Northeast is a petri dish allowing for this type of spread," New York said. "Besides, I imagine there were quite a few boys and girls from Philadelphia running all up and down Broad Street during that parade *you* authorized on Saturday."

The mayor narrowed his eyes and was silent for a moment. Then he said, "It's just the damn flu, for crying out loud."

"Mr. Mayor," Wilmer cut in, "this is no ordinary—"

"We all get it every year," Mayor Smith continued. "Runny noses for three or four days and then it's over."

Boston and New York exchanged looks, and Boston briefly crossed his eyes with annoyance.

"I can assure you, Mayor," New York said, "that I—that *we*—have never seen anything like this sickness. And you haven't, either."

Mayor Smith shook his head.

"Have you seen bodies turning blue? Shooting blood out of the mouth, the nose, and both ears?" Boston asked the mayor pointedly. "Have you seen a person go from perfectly fine to dead on the ground within hours? Because you will."

"In any case," New York continued, "it's here now, and you'd better get that into your thick skull. No amount of bribery or vote rigging or whatever it is you're up to these days can change that fact."

Wilmer saw the mayor tighten his grip on his pen. It seemed New York had been reading the papers.

"Right," Wilmer said, before things got out of hand. "The surgeon general has asked the Red Cross to mobilize and help us fight this. I talked to the chief of the Philadelphia-Delaware chapter and he said he'd do all he could."

Wilmer didn't mention what else the chief had said: "The primary responsibility really rests with the community board of health." Meaning Wilmer. But what could Wilmer do? A silent killer was now moving among them. How do you fight an invisible enemy that has already invaded your home?

"Mayor," he began, "we'll need money. As much money as the city can spare."

The mayor nodded. "I'll give you the whole damn emergency fund. Just stop this thing."

Wilmer knew the next thing he said wouldn't sit too well with the mayor on a normal day. But this wasn't a normal day.

"We must put a stop to any public gatherings," he said. "Close the schools; close the churches, the courts, the theaters."

The mayor nodded very slowly and sighed.

"And no more funerals," Wilmer continued. "There are too many dead now."

---

In the lobby at Donohue Funeral Home on South Street, Barium stood over his mother's body, which was covered by a white bedsheet and lay on a gurney. He was glad he couldn't see her discolored face. He wanted to forget he'd ever seen her like that.

Barium stepped back, dodging the sheet-wrapped bodies that lined the floor of the lobby. He moved through the path that was kept clear so that mourners could make their way to the chapel area, where services for the bodies in the hallway would be conducted. A line of families—adults and children, some sitting on the ground, some leaning against the building—stretched around the corner to the back of the funeral home. Each time the next family was called and led into the funeral home, the line inched forward slightly.

A man with a white medical mask over his mouth and nose opened the doors to the chapel, gesturing for the next family to enter. Presiding over the services, at the far end of the small room stood Father Joseph Murphy. It was his twentieth funeral of the day. The man in the mask pushed the gurney carrying Barium's mother into the chapel and handed Father Murphy a piece of paper with a name on it: Sylvia Epp.

Barium stepped into the chapel, followed closely by his aunt Selma and uncle Mike—Sylvia's sister and her husband. They lived on the same block of South Street and were now Barium's only family. Aunt Selma squeezed her nephew's hand and cried.

Barium grasped Aunt Selma's hand back and stared ahead at his mother's body. He felt strangely grateful that he had this hand to cling to now. What would he have done if his aunt and uncle weren't in Philly? Who would take in a poor teenager whose mother had just died from a highly contagious, often fatal illness?

"Almighty God and Father," Father Murphy prayed. "It is our certain faith that your Son, who died on the cross, was raised from the dead, the first fruits of all of who have fallen asleep."

Father Murphy paused, and Barium, who hadn't closed his eyes, looked up and absently watched the priest as he prayed.

"Grant that through this mystery your servant Sylvia, who has gone to her rest in Christ, may share in the joy of his resurrection . . ."

Barium could hear Father Murphy's words, but it was as if he were listening to a foreign language. None of the words made sense—they were just collections of syllables. Then one phrase broke through his consciousness—*gone to her rest*. His mother was dead. Yesterday she'd made him eggs, scolded him about his homework, and laughed at his imitation of his teacher's heavily accented voice. Today she was wrapped in a bedsheet and being talked about by some man who didn't even know her.

Father Murphy continued his prayer, but Barium could no longer listen. He shut his eyes tight to keep his tears at bay as the priest's voice droned on mournfully. All Barium wanted right now was for Father Murphy to say the one word that would tell him this wretched business was over. A few minutes and many words later, he finally heard it.

"Amen," Father Murphy said.

Aunt Selma let go of Barium's hand to rub away her tears. She covered her face with both hands and sobbed, her head shaking. Uncle Mike put his arm around her, and Barium stepped away from them and crept up to the body. He ran his fingers along the top of the sheet, feeling for his mother's hand. Finding it, he clasped it and allowed a few tears to escape his eyelids before blinking them into a film that glazed over his eyes.

The doors of the chapel opened, and Barium heard the commotion of the next family scrambling to get in. He hesitantly let go of his mother's hand and turned to rejoin his aunt and uncle, who were thanking Father Murphy. Where his hand had just been holding his mother's through the sheet, there was now a yellowish blue stain.

An attendant approached to lead them out the back door. Outside, the line of mourners waiting to bid farewell to loved ones was winding around the funeral home. A few of the people in line lifted their heads to look at the departing participants of the previous funeral, then lowered them again and took a few steps as the line slowly moved forward.

———•◆•———

Wilmer sat at his desk at city hall with his head in his hands. After another long day of talking to hospital directors, doctors, nurses, business owners, government workers, and Red Cross officials, he knew that it was all over. The city of Philadelphia was being hit by an asteroid of an epidemic, one that had already smashed into New York and Boston. Of course, he didn't—couldn't—fully voice his pessimism to Mayor Smith, who could only handle so much bad news before he started firing people. But Wilmer knew. People were going to continue to get sick, and the deaths would continue to pile up. Until they didn't. Until the illness had run its course. He was powerless to stop it.

And one other thing he knew: the Liberty Loan Parade had placed a giant bull's-eye smack in the middle of the City of Brotherly Love. He had a sinking feeling that what Philadelphia was about to experience would make the stories coming out of New York and Boston look like a silly plot from one of those Rover Boys adventure books.

The phone rang.

"Krusen," Wilmer said warily.

"Dr. Krusen, this is Monsignor Drumgoole over at St. Charles." It was the friendliest voice Wilmer had heard all day. "I trust you are holding up all right?"

"Yes, Monsignor, as well as can be expected, I suppose."

"And no symptoms of this dreadful thing?"

"Not a one, thank the Lord." Wilmer knocked on his desk with his knuckles.

A sign at Philadelphia's Naval Aircraft Factory warns of the dangers of spitting.

"I'm very glad to hear it. Now it is my understanding that you are seeking volunteers to help bury the dead."

"Yes, Monsignor. As you've no doubt heard, we're having an awful time disposing of . . . dealing with the increasing number of bodies. They're being left in the street, on front porches. It's a foul business. Especially over at Holy Cross, the fellows can't keep up. Bodies that we've managed to transport out there are now piling up at the cemetery with no one to bury them. But every cemetery is overwhelmed with bodies—Holy Sepulchre, New Cathedral."

"I see," Monsignor Drumgoole said. "Well, there's nothing for it but to have a team of our students come out and assist, is there?"

"It would be a great help."

"I'll communicate the need to our boys at the earliest opportunity. These poor souls must have a proper burial."

"Yes," Wilmer replied. He wasn't about to tell the monsignor that there would likely be nothing "proper" about these burials. They would be quick and dirty. There would be no service, no time for more than silent prayers whispered by the seminary students as they dug the graves. "Thank you, Monsignor."

Wilmer hung up the phone and exhaled loudly. He looked at his notebook, where he kept all the latest numbers. Nearly three hundred people had died in the previous forty-eight hours. And reports were continuing to come in of more deaths and more pleas for help. This sickness was outpacing the city's ability to handle all the victims, who were being cast aside like so much garbage.

Wilmer picked up his copy of the *Philadelphia Inquirer* and reread the headline on the bottom of page 5: "Scientists Make Progress Identifying Pathogen Causing Influenza."

Wilmer shook his head glumly. "Doesn't matter," he muttered. There was no vaccine that could be produced fast enough to drag Philadelphia out of the asteroid's path. The epidemic had reached a terminal phase—it would only stop when enough susceptible people were infected.

He had no power, no control. It would end when it ended.

Wilmer looked over at the giant placard leaning against his office wall. It was the latest public health poster, hot off the presses and being hung all over town.

"Spitting Equals Death."

⸻

Barium sat down, let go of his suitcase, and looked out onto South Street from the main room of his aunt and uncle's second-floor apartment. He still wore his white cotton shirt and black pants, the only nice articles of clothing he owned. He'd shined his scuffed-up dress shoes, using his own spit and a sock. He thought his mother would have approved of the way he'd dressed himself.

He couldn't believe how quickly her funeral had passed. And how they'd just been pushed out of the funeral home afterward.

"What are they gonna do with her body?" he'd asked his aunt and uncle on the walk home.

Aunt Selma and Uncle Mike had looked uneasily at each other.

"They'll be taking her to Holy Cross, Barry," Aunt Selma had said. "But not until they're done with services for all those others that were in the lobby."

"When do we go to Holy Cross for the burial?" Barium had asked.

Silence.

"We don't," Uncle Mike had said finally.

"Why not?"

"Barry . . ." Aunt Selma had sighed. "There won't be a cemetery service. We said good-bye at the funeral home. There are too many bodies to have a burial for everyone."

Barium's lips had quivered.

"We'll go find out where they've put her after all this is over, honey," she had continued, stroking his hair. "There are just . . . too many."

Barium couldn't shake the image of his mother shoved into a corner of the funeral parlor, like a piece of trash kicked to the curb.

Through the window Barium saw Harriet and Harry out on the street outside their apartment, a few doors over from

Aunt Selma and Uncle Mike's. Barium watched as Harry kicked a balled-up newspaper down the street and Harriet yelled at him to watch out for any passing cars.

Barium felt an overwhelming urge to join them. "I'm going to go say hi to the Milani kids," he said to his aunt and uncle.

"Barry, are you sure you want to?" Aunt Selma asked. "They'll have all kinds of questions about your mother. Maybe better to stay put."

Barium hesitated for a moment before opening the door. "I'll just say hi, see how they're doing. Make sure no one's sick at their house." He closed the door behind him and bounded down to the street.

"Barium!" Harry couldn't contain his excitement. "Hey! You want to play trash ball with us?"

"Hi, Barium," Harriet said, waving awkwardly. "We heard about your mom . . ."

Barium nodded and looked away. "Everything okay in your family?"

"Yeah, but our mother won't let us come outside but for a few minutes a day now. And only right outside the apartment," Harry said.

"Actually, she should be calling us in any second now," Harriet said, worriedly looking at the first-floor window for her mother's face.

"Kids!" Spotting the children talking to Barium outside, Mrs. Milani shouted from the main door of the tenement building. "Harry, Harriet, time to come in." She looked at Barium warily but didn't speak to him.

"Aw, Mom—"

"Now!"

Harry and Harriet slumped toward the door, saying good-bye to Barium. Mrs. Milani didn't take her eyes off their young neighbor.

"Hi, Mrs. Milani," Barium said, trying to sound breezy. He stepped forward, and Mrs. Milani flinched.

"Hello," she said, rushing the children inside. She stepped back and started pulling the door to close it. "We were very sorry to hear about your mother."

"Thank you." Barium stooped to pick up the little trash ball Harry had been kicking around. He held it out to Mrs. Milani.

"I'm sorry, Barium," Mrs. Milani said sharply. "I just . . . we can't." She shut the door, leaving Barium standing on the sidewalk with the balled-up newspaper in his hand.

He gazed at the window of the Milanis' apartment, listening to the bustling, lively household inside. Little Harry poked his head up and waved to Barium, then disappeared into the apartment.

# 3

# SPASMS

HOLMESBURG EMERGENCY HOSPITAL No. 1 in South Philadelphia was encircled by crowds of sick people, some wrapped in blankets, some only in their shirtsleeves but soaking in sweat. Their guttural moans, gurgled breathing, and labored, forlorn conversations—not only in English but also in Italian, Spanish, Yiddish, and German—filled the air. There weren't enough beds inside to accommodate the number of patients arriving every day, so newcomers had to stand—or sit or lie—on the sidewalk and wait. Wait for some poor soul inside to die and free up a bed.

A few blocks away a young pregnant woman stumbled down the sidewalk toward the hospital, coughing and stopping after every few steps to catch her breath. Her hands were clasped around the underside of her large belly as if she were trying to keep it attached to her body. She leaned against a street sign and coughed until she spat out something yellow and brown, then moved on. She was slick with sweat, her clothes grimy and stuck to her body, her hair disheveled.

Seeing a man on the other side of the street, she stumbled into the road, hoarsely calling, "Help! Help! Water!" She took one arm from her belly and pointed at her mouth as she cried out. The man on the opposite sidewalk, a mask tied tightly over his mouth and nose, looked at her and jogged away, darting around the corner. "Help me!" she cried weakly. "Water." Another man and woman, also wearing masks, rushed past her, as though she weren't there. She rushed toward them with one arm stretched out, screaming, "Water! Please!" But they outpaced her and disappeared down a side street.

"Please," she cried softly. "Please."

The woman crossed to the other side of the street and leaned on a telephone pole papered with health department warnings. "Cover Your Mouth When You Cough!" one instructed.

She looked at the throng of sick people crowded around the hospital's main building. Exhausted, her body aching with every tiny movement, she took a deep, labored breath and then jerked herself forward. Ignoring the line of people, she walked right around them, straight for the entrance. Gaining strength as she moved, she increased her wobbly pace as people shouted at her to get in line.

"Hey! Line starts back there!"

"What makes you so important?"

She reached out for the nurse standing there guarding the entrance. The nurse, a mask over her nose and mouth, looked up just as the woman fell to her knees, coughing and gurgling.

"Oh God!" the woman cried. "Please, please help me!" She looked down at her belly, her face full of agony. She reached out to the nurse, who backed away, shouting into the building for a doctor. The nurse stepped back out and looked at the woman with fear and pity. From behind her Wilmer Krusen emerged, carrying a clipboard, his face also covered with a mask.

On her knees, with one hand on the pavement and the other holding her stomach, the woman struggled to breathe, inhaling slowly and emitting a thick hissing sound. She finally collapsed face-first onto the sidewalk.

Wilmer rushed over to the woman and knelt down, gazing sadly at her pregnant belly as her hand slid off it and slapped against the pavement. He called out to an orderly for help, and the two men lifted the woman and carried her inside.

"Hey!" an elderly man waiting in line yelled at Wilmer as he passed. The old man coughed and spat. "Hey, why are you taking her inside? We've been here for hours!" The door swung closed, and the man cursed and coughed again.

"Why does *she* get help? She's already dead!"

———•◦•———

At the library of St. Charles Borromeo Seminary in Lower Merion, eight miles north of Philadelphia, Tim closed his theology books and placed them in his bag. After many hours of study, he was ready to unwind with the newspaper. He opened yesterday's copy of the *Philadelphia Gazette,* reading through the war coverage dominating the front page. He ran his eyes over the stories of the French and American offensive against the Germans in the Argonne Forest, the recent armistice signed between Bulgaria and the Allies, and the public events to raise money for the war effort in cities across America. He couldn't remember the last time he had read a story on the front page that wasn't somehow related to the Great War.

He absently turned the pages, trying to find something to read that didn't involve violence and death, when a page toward

**Officials in major cities feared possible unrest during the epidemic. Here police officers patrol Seattle.**

the back stopped him cold. It was a list of people in and around Philadelphia who had died from influenza. He knew about this particular flu and that there were a worrying number of cases in Boston—but how had he not known that there were so many victims in Philadelphia? He scanned an article below the list of names, which offered the grim news that the city's mortality rate was the worst in its history.

"Conditions in South Philadelphia are worse than at any time in my experience," the article quoted a local politician as saying. "The people are panic stricken, the doctors overworked, and many pharmacies short of the necessary drugs."

This sent a shiver down Tim's spine. He thought back to a few days before, when he'd spent all day in Philadelphia with

Thomas, Leo, and Richard, watching the Liberty Loan Parade, enjoying a few beers at a tavern on Broad Street, walking along the crowded streets while taking in the scenery, and soaking up the sunshine and the carnival-like atmosphere. Richard had stayed in town to see family while Tim, Leo, and Thomas had taken the last train back to Lower Merion, sneaking guiltily back to their dorms, having missed Saturday Mass. He wondered if Richard or someone in his family was sick—he hadn't seen him since. Tim shot up out of his chair, grabbed his satchel, and hurried out of the library.

"Good evening, Master Buckley," Sister Katherine said to Tim as she overtook him in the covered walkway leading from the library to the dorms.

"Good evening, Sister Katherine. I'm looking for Thomas Ryan and Leo Naylor—have you seen either of them this evening?"

"I've just seen Master Ryan go into the chapel, as a matter of fact," the nun replied. "I expect you've heard the dreadful news." Tim noticed now that she'd been crying.

"News? What news?"

"Oh, Master Buckley, I'm sorry. I didn't mean to . . ."

Tim didn't wait for her to finish. He darted across the campus green toward the chapel.

———•◆•———

Wilmer entered the makeshift morgue of the emergency hospital, his white medical mask covering his nose and mouth. Not much bigger than a closet, this was one of only a few spaces on the first floor where the dead could be taken so that their cots could be made available to other patients. His entrance startled Sister Agnes, one of the nuns helping to care for the sick in emergency hospitals across the city. She was praying over the body of a recently deceased patient.

"I'm sorry, Sister," Wilmer stammered, backing away. "Didn't mean to interrupt."

"It's all right." She crossed herself and stood. "I've finished. I must return to the sickrooms."

"Sister Agnes," Wilmer interjected.

"Yes, Dr. Krusen?"

"I imagine you are quite . . . overwhelmed."

Sister Agnes nodded.

"Please be assured, I'm endeavoring to get you more help, as soon as possible. I've put in requests for additional assistance here at Holmesburg. God willing, there will be some recruits arriving to relieve you sisters so you can get away from this . . . sickness. And get some rest."

"Thank you, Dr. Krusen," Sister Agnes answered. "We'll be grateful for any help that arrives. In the meantime, there's God's work to do. There are so many suffering."

Wilmer nodded. "Thank you, Sister," he said as she slipped out into the hallway.

He gazed at the person she had been praying over and around the small space now overrun with the dead. All around him lay bodies of flu victims, their white wrappings discolored by streaks of yellowish brown, black, and dark red. Wilmer backed out of the room and stepped back into the hallway, moving from one ghastly—though mercifully tiny—enclave into an even larger one.

The epidemic had spun out of control. The bodies in the little room he'd just left were the lucky ones. The halls he now moved through were thick with the putrid stench of death and lined with bodies that hadn't even been afforded the dignity of a sheet. Some, completely cold, had given up the ghost days before. Others were still warm, their lives only recently extinguished. Every single body was the color of a violent bruise—a ghoulish blue-black hue. Alive, these Philadelphians were white, black, or brown—now they were all united. One single race of the dead.

Tim raced across campus, not stopping until he reached the chapel entrance. Pausing briefly to catch his breath, he opened the doors and stepped inside the dimly lit sanctuary. Pushing through the vestibule doors, he entered the chapel nave and saw Thomas kneeling at the altar at the far end, his short black hair seeming to undulate in the flickers of candlelight.

"Thomas," Tim whispered as he moved down the aisle. Thomas was as still as a statue, head bowed, hands clasped together in prayer, elbows resting on the altar.

"Thomas." Tim padded up to the altar and crouched beside him, putting his hand on Thomas's shoulder. Thomas opened his eyes and lifted his head, as if awaking from a dream.

"What on earth happened?" Tim asked.

Thomas looked over at Tim. "It's Richard—he never came back from town."

"Oh. Is his family sick?"

Thomas nodded. "Yes, they all are. And then Richard got sick, too."

"Well, I'm sure he'll be fine—his father's a doctor. Let's go call him now. Come on . . ."

"No, Tim. We can't."

"'Course we can. We'll use the phone in the dorm."

"Tim, Richard is dead."

———————

Harry and Harriet Milani sat by their living-room window, looking outside at the empty street. Harry pressed his face against the glass, making his nose into a pig snout. He turned his head slightly to make sure his sister saw.

"Harry, stop being silly," Harriet scolded after trying to ignore him for a few seconds. "Look," she said. They watched as a middle-aged woman in front of one of the apartments across the street tied a piece of black crepe to the doorknob of the front door, gazed at it for a moment, then slipped back inside.

"Her husband, I think," Harriet mumbled.

"He got sick?" Harry asked.

"Yeah, he got sick and now he's in heaven."

"Are all those people in heaven?" Harry asked. He pointed to the row of apartments lining the street, almost all of which had crepe paper hanging from the doors to signify a death inside— white paper for children, black for adults, and gray for the elderly.

"Is Daddy gonna go there, too?"

A loud series of coughs erupted from the bedroom a few feet away.

Harriet didn't answer her brother. She wished she hadn't even brought up heaven.

Mr. Milani had fallen ill the previous day, and after arriving home from his job at the munitions factory, had gone straight to bed. Overnight he had transformed from their robust and playful father into a weak and shivering rag doll. Mrs. Milani had been nursing him all day—applying vapor rub, giving him

A clothesline inside a crowded Philadelphia tenement apartment, circa 1910

aspirin, preparing a homemade whiskey remedy, and keeping a wet cloth on his forehead, which she periodically came out to the kitchen to wash and reset. She had forbidden the children to come into the room—instead, she set up little sleeping spaces for them on the floor of the sitting room, the only other full room in the apartment. Harry and Harriet hadn't left the room in two days.

All of a sudden the bedroom door opened, and Mrs. Milani emerged.

"Can we see Daddy?" Harry whispered.

Mrs. Milani shook her head. "Not now, honey, he's sleeping. Daddy's very sick." She padded into the tiny kitchen to wash her hands. After drying them on a dingy towel, she untied her mask and turned back to the children.

"I'm going to go sit with him again. He's having trouble breathing, and Mommy's got to make sure he doesn't choke on . . ." She stopped, having said too much.

"Make sure . . . ?" Harriet said. Harry looked at his sister and then up at his mother, his lips starting to tremble.

"Make sure he doesn't cough so much that he chokes," Mrs. Milani said. "You know, Harry, when you can't stop coughing?"

Harry nodded.

"Well, Daddy's just having a lot of coughing spells. Mommy's going to sit with him now in case he needs anything."

Harry nodded again, and Harriet took his hand. Mrs. Milani opened the bedroom door and closed it quickly behind her.

"Hey, Harriet!" Harry said, pointing out the window. "Don't you know her from school?"

Harriet ran to the window. Sure enough, there was her friend Susanna, walking toward their building and waving. She was wearing a white mask over her mouth and nose, and as she approached the apartment's window, she loosened it and let it hang around her neck. They could see that she had an agitated look on her face.

"What is she doing here?" Harriet wondered aloud. She hadn't seen Susanna since the city had closed the schools the other day.

Susanna reached the window and signaled for Harriet to come outside. Harriet shook her head and mouthed, "Can't."

Susanna rolled her eyes and pointed to the door of the building. Harriet crept out into the hall and over to the entrance, with Harry following quickly behind her. She opened the door just a sliver—her mother had told her not to let anyone inside.

"What's going on?" Harriet asked, peeking around the door.

"It's . . . you just have to see it. You won't believe me."

"Have to see what?" Harry asked suspiciously, standing on his tiptoes and sticking his head out from behind his sister.

Susanna turned her face to where South Street intersected Broad Street a few blocks west.

"Up there," she said. "Near the funeral home."

"What's up there?" Harriet demanded in an irritated whisper.

"It's a wagon. Full of dead bodies."

Harriet whirled around to see if Harry had heard. His wide eyes told her he had.

---

Wilmer had only intended to stop by Holmesburg for a few minutes, to see what was needed in terms of supplies, volunteers, and medical personnel. But the place was so understaffed that he had drafted himself to care for patients.

There were no available doctors or nurses in Philadelphia who weren't already working at other hospitals, so he had had to send out desperate pleas through the Red Cross, newspapers, and flyers asking for retired and out-of-town doctors, nurses, and student residents to just show up at their closest hospital

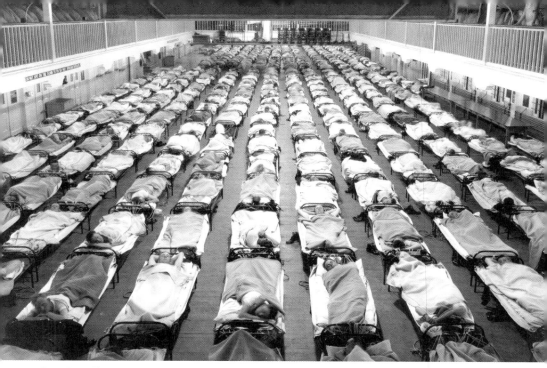

A makeshift sleeping area in the Drill Hall of the Naval Training Station in San Francisco captures the essence of what many emergency hospitals looked like during the epidemic.

and help in any way they could. In South Philadelphia, plagued as it was by the overcrowding and unhygienic conditions of tenement life, this epidemic had found a horrifically fertile breeding ground. The influenza was eating the district alive.

Wilmer turned a corner to exit through the back door and immediately stopped in his tracks. At his feet lay the body of a woman. Even through death's disguise he recognized her. He had brought her inside himself when she had collapsed at the hospital door that morning. In a room full of other mortally ill souls, he'd tried to revive her and save the baby she carried. He had accomplished neither.

After closing her eyelids, he'd asked Sister Agnes to help him place the woman on the floor of the hallway so he could free up the bed for another patient. As they had carried the woman out and placed her on the floor of the hall, Wilmer's eyes had filled with tears.

He now stepped over the woman's body and exited the building, keeping his head down as he walked to his car. Desperately ill people still waiting in line outside screamed at him as he passed, begging for their lives.

———

Harriet popped her head into the bedroom. Her parents' bed was against the wall, facing the door. They were both asleep now—Mommy curled up next to Daddy, her head on his chest. Harriet backed away and closed the door.

"They're asleep," she said to her brother. "Let's go quickly."

Harriet and Harry raced out to meet Susanna, who waved them on toward Broad Street. The two siblings followed her up to the corner by the funeral home. Out in front of the building were wagons piled high with bodies wrapped in dirty sheets.

"Those are all bodies," Susanna whispered.

Harry ran up to the first wagon to get a closer look.

"Harry!" Harriet shouted after him. "What are you doing?"

He had to see one. He couldn't help himself. He had to see.

Harry stopped about a foot from the wagon and stared. One of the sheet-wrapped bodies protruded off the edge. Harry stepped closer, holding his breath. He took the sheet and whipped it up.

A dark blue face—man or woman, black or white, old or young, it was impossible to tell—stared at him vacantly. A worm wriggled out of its open mouth.

Harry screamed and ran all the way home.

# 4

# THE SICK HALL

Monsignor Drumgoole looked around the small mess hall, where he'd assembled all the seminary students at St. Charles. The young men gazed at him soberly, periodically looking around at each other to make sure what they heard had really just been said. It sounded like some ghoulish story from the Middle Ages: an inexplicably fast-moving illness, bodies piled upon bodies in the streets, entire towns decimated. A plague.

"The overburdened staff at the Holy Cross Cemetery is in dire need of our help," Monsignor Drumgoole continued. "There are, sadly, not enough still living to properly bury the dead."

Tim, sitting at a table near the front of the room, looked over at Thomas and Leo, made eye contact, and nodded at them. Thomas nodded back, but Leo just stared.

"It will be a grim task, make no mistake." Monsignor Drumgoole sighed. "There will not be words to describe some of the things you might see. I say this not to frighten you but to prepare you. I've already given leave to all the sisters here at St. Charles who are not needed for the most essential domestic tasks. They have begun scattering about Philadelphia to visit hospitals and homes and offer care, comfort, and God's love to those souls who have been touched by this horrid illness. But while the sisters administer to the living, we must steel ourselves to administer to the dead."

Shocked murmurs spread over the mess hall.

"So I'm asking for volunteers," Monsignor Drumgoole continued. "The first troupe of thirty will go this afternoon, and we'll assess the cemetery's needs. The volunteer list is posted at the back. We want to assemble the first group quickly, while there are still a few hours of daylight left, so please make haste."

The monsignor nodded and walked out, leaving the young men to their worried discussions.

"I'll go sign all our names," Tim said to Thomas and Leo. "We should all go together, out of respect for Richard."

"Yes, fine by me," Thomas said. "Leo?"

"Yes," Leo said, though his face betrayed hesitation. "Yes."

Tim and Thomas exchanged looks.

"You're sure, Leo?" Tim asked. "Thomas and I can go if you don't feel up to it."

"No," Leo assured them. "You're right—we should do it for Richard."

Tim sprang up from his seat and stepped to the back where the sign-up sheet was posted.

———◆———

Harriet caught up to Harry at the entrance to their building.

"Harry, I'm sorry," she said, taking him by the shoulders and pulling him in for a hug. "I shouldn't have let you look. I wasn't thinking."

Harry was crying. His sister wiped the tears from his eyes.

"Sometimes your big sister is just a big dummy." She smiled. "Come on. Let's go inside and see about making some dinner."

The children tiptoed back inside their tiny apartment. Harriet headed straight for her parents' bedroom door and poked her head into the darkened room, where she saw the silhouettes of her parents resting.

"It's okay, they're still sleeping," she said. She and Harry flopped down on the living-room couch, which faced the window looking out onto the trash-strewn street. Both of them had closed their eyes and had begun to drift into sleep when there came a knock at the window.

Harriet sat up and looked around. It was Barium, pressing his face against the window to try to get a better look inside the apartment. He saw Harriet and pointed to the entrance, indicating he was coming in. Harriet scurried over to the door and, again, opened it only a sliver. Barium was a friend, of course, but after his mother died, Mrs. Milani had been adamant that Harry and Harriet not be around him—he might have the illness himself, she'd said.

"Hi, Barium," Harriet said as he strode down the hallway toward her.

"Hi there, Harriet. Everything okay?"

"Oh, yes, we're fine."

Barium could only see Harriet's lips, her nose, and part of one of her eyes, so narrowly was she holding open the door.

"Well, I heard Harry screaming a few minutes ago, running down the street," Barium said.

"Yeah," Harriet said, rolling her eyes. "I bet everyone in Philadelphia heard it."

"Hi, Barium!" A grinning Harry yanked the door wide open, knocking his sister in the head as he did it.

"Ow! Harry!"

"Oh, Harriet, can I help?" Barium asked. He stepped into their apartment, reaching out to steady her.

"No!" Harriet blurted out, putting a hand out to block Barium's entrance. Barium took a tiny step back into the hallway.

"I'm sorry, Barium, we just . . ." She trailed off. "My mother says that . . ."

Barium nodded. "It's okay." He looked over at Harry, who was still grinning. "Hi, buddy! You doing okay?"

Harry's smile disappeared. "We saw dead bodies."

Harriet nodded. "Yeah. Harry saw something he probably shouldn't have."

"Oh, the wagons up by the funeral home, huh?" Barium said. "Well, I just wanted to come check on you. How are your parents?"

"Daddy's sick," Harry said quickly.

Barium's face fell. "Really? How long has he been sick?"

"Came home sick from work yesterday," Harriet explained. "Been in bed ever since."

"And where's your mother?"

"She's in there with him most of the time."

"Trying to fix him!" Harry chimed in.

Barium stepped toward the doorway, concerned. "When's the last time you checked on them?"

"I looked in on them about an hour ago," Harriet said, hesitantly raising her hand again.

"Do you need me to go try to get some medicine?" Barium asked. "What's your mother using?"

"I don't know," Harriet said. "Some stuff she rubs on him. And she's got him wearing a string of camphor around his neck."

"Hmm," Barium said thoughtfully. He didn't want to frighten them, but he knew from experience how quickly things could go from bad to absolute worst. "Why don't I just pop into the room and ask your mother what she needs?"

"But she said we shouldn't let you in here," Harry said.

Harriet rolled her eyes at her brother's lack of tact.

"No, it's okay," Barium said. "I understand why she said that. But I'm not sick so far, and neither are my aunt and uncle. This sickness comes fast—if I'd caught what my mother had, I'd already be—"

He stopped himself. Harriet's face was drawn with worried lines, and Harry looked like he usually did—uncertain.

"Anyway," Barium continued, "I'll just chat with your mother real quick-like, and then go down to the store and bring you whatever you need. You can come with me!"

Harriet hesitated, knowing what her mother would say. But the thought of having someone to talk to besides her baby brother was too tempting. She stepped back from the doorway.

"Okay, you can come in."

Barium stepped into the apartment. "You two put on your masks and go wait on the sidewalk. I'll be right out," he said. Harry and Harriet did what he said, while Barium approached the bedroom door.

He knocked lightly. There was no answer, so he knocked again.

"Mrs. Milani?" he said. "It's Barium Epp, your neighbor." Still no answer. Barium could hear Harry outside, lecturing his sister that she would get in big trouble for letting Barium inside.

Barium turned the doorknob and entered, gingerly closing the door behind him. The room was dark, though he could make out the black shapes of the Milanis on the bed. He stood in the dark for a moment to let his eyes adjust to the darkness. Seeing the shape of a lamp over in the corner, he crept over to turn it on, stumbling on a pair of shoes on the floor.

Blinking in the sudden brightness, Barium could see Mr. Milani on the right, lying on his back. His face was darkened like a sky ready to explode with rain, and his nose and mouth were covered with dark red blood. Barium recognized the horrible color. He looked at Mrs. Milani, curled up beside her husband, her head on his chest. Her face was the same purplish blue.

They were both gone.

<hr />

Sister Katherine stood all alone in a dimly lit changing closet at Emergency Hospital No. 8 on South Broad Street. She looked down at the long white gown she had draped over her normal nun's habit—it covered her from shoulders to shoe tops. The last item she needed to complete her volunteer-nurse uniform was the gauze mask, which she pulled out of a supply box and fitted over her mouth and nose. She lifted a rosary and kissed it through the mask, then whispered a quiet prayer as she prepared to leave the safety of the closet and emerge into a room filled with—if the stories from her fellow nuns were to be believed—unimaginable horrors.

She opened the door, and immediately the sounds and scents of the ill descended upon her. Head down, she entered the sick hall and walked to the far corner, where Rachel, the nurse in charge, had instructed her to come so she could be taught how to bathe a patient.

All around her swirled the moans and cries of the dying. Patients reached bony arms out to her from their cots as she moved past. Nausea crept over her while she walked, and she murmured prayers to stave off the feeling that she herself was about to be sick.

"Lord, steel me. I'm here to do your work. Keep all of us in your care, O Father."

A guttural bellowing filled the hall. Looking up, she saw Rachel run toward her and then dart to the right, where two nurses were trying to restrain a male patient who was flailing around in front of the hospital office and grasping at anything within reach. The man was screaming words at the top of his voice, and as Sister Katherine crept over to Rachel, she could make out some of what he was saying.

"Gotta catch the kaiser! Let go o' me!"

"William!" Rachel shouted. "William! Calm down, William!"

The nurses were struggling to keep him restrained as he spat and snarled. A male orderly arrived and held William's hands behind his back. Rachel quickly ducked into the supply closet and emerged a few moments later with a leather medical case.

"The kaiser ain't afeared! He ain't afeared o' you! But he 'feared o' me! He know I'm the only one! Only one can catch 'im!"

"No, William, the kaiser is nowhere near here. You are in the hospital on Broad Street, and you are very ill."

William squirmed as Rachel opened the leather case and began preparing a needle. When William caught sight of the needle, he began to scream anew.

"You workin' for the kaiser! She workin' for the kaiser!" He tried to wrestle free from the orderly as Rachel placed the tip of the needle against his arm.

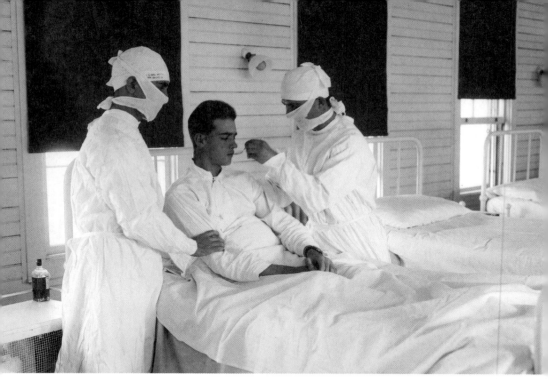

Doctors and nurses—including those pictured here in New Orleans, Louisiana—took precautions when treating patients.

"Hold him tight," she said to the orderly before slowly pulling the needle back, aiming it like a dart, and then plunging it into William's arm. As she pressed the morphine into him, William wailed and wriggled his head violently, his eyes clenched shut.

Sister Katherine watched Rachel administer the drug to William. He stopped yelling and squirming, and one of the nurses soon took his limp hand and led him back over to his cot. He dragged his feet behind her, not saying a word. When they arrived at his cot, the nurse held him as a second nurse wound rolled-up sheets around him, binding him securely to the cot so that he couldn't hurt anyone if he had another episode.

Sister Katherine looked around, wondering where she should go. A man on a cot beside her lay gasping, his eyes and mouth wide open. He reached out to her and moaned words that she couldn't understand. On either side of him were two men lying perfectly still, wrapped in white sheets.

"Those men are dead," the orderly said matter-of-factly. "That's why they're wrapped. That sad wretch in the middle will be gone soon. Gotta get some help to move them—too many for me to handle." He padded away to find one of his fellow orderlies.

Rachel reemerged from the office where she'd deposited the morphine case. "Poor William—he's been in a state all day. So, Sister Katherine, are you ready to learn all about giving these poor souls a bath?"

———————

Barium stepped out of the Milanis' apartment building and onto the filthy pavement. While waiting for him Harriet and Harry had drawn a hopscotch course on the sidewalk with chalk, and now they were jumping through it. Behind them on South Street, a wagon full of bodies rolled past. Barium heard someone weeping in an apartment across the street, though the sound didn't disturb the Milani children's concentration on their game. He watched as Harriet gracefully hopped on one foot then two, one foot then two, then two again, then one, then one again, then out. Each hop was immaculate and perfectly placed, and he expected that Harry would turn in a clumsier performance.

Harry stepped up to the course and hopped into the air: one foot, then two, then one foot and another foot plus a hand, then two feet, then one foot, then a surprising leap beyond the next squares and out of the course and onto his backside. Harry giggled, and Harriet laughed and rolled her eyes at her brother's rule-breaking.

Barium smiled at the two children, whose lives he knew would never be the same. He wanted to stretch out this time, when they didn't know the truth and could laugh and play without realizing that darkness had already descended. He wasn't sure what he was going to do, but he did know one thing: he couldn't allow them to see their parents that way. He'd have to tell them the truth soon. But for now—just right now—he wanted to let their blissful ignorance last.

Harry saw Barium and leaped back up.

"Barium, can we get some candy at the store?"

"Harry," Harriet scolded, "we're going to get medicine!"

"It's okay." Barium smiled. "We can get some candy, too. Might as well, huh?"

Barium reached out his hand and Harry seized it, leading Barium to the corner store as Harriet walked behind.

# "Do You See the Angels?"

"It'll be grisly work, I'm afraid," the superintendent of Holy Cross Cemetery said to Tim. They stood outside the office overlooking the sloping greenery of the grounds. "But I imagine you knew that when you signed up."

Tim nodded. "Yes, sir. We're here to commend as many poor souls as we can—to the ground and to the Lord." He looked around the grounds in the afternoon light. "We'll divide into groups and get as much done as we can before the last train back."

"Shovels are over there," the superintendent said, pointing to a shed with its doors hanging open. "And other things that we'll have to use as shovels. Feel free to get creative."

"Thank you, sir." Tim tipped his cap and backed away. When he had been chosen as the group leader, he hadn't been sure he was up to such a fearsome task as organizing a team of body buriers. He himself had never even attended a family funeral. When he first set foot on the cemetery grounds and saw so many bodies stacked in trucks, carts, and wagons, and piled up in front of the office, he breathed a quick, quiet prayer.

Tim, Thomas, and Leo approached the other volunteers from St. Charles, who stood waiting for instructions. They walked among the corpses strewn on the ground. Each had been tagged by a coroner, nurse, doctor, or funeral director—whoever had taken possession of the body after death. Here was one wrapped in a sheet, its black, bloated feet sticking out at the bottom. There was a young woman, her mouth open and her jaw jutting out, both arms angled in front of her dark blue face, frozen in a pose of gasping—literally reaching—for air. A boy near her, dressed in dirty pajamas, was the same dark blue color. Beside the boy lay a man in his underwear, his body greenish and swollen like a balloon, maggots wriggling under his nostrils and around his eyes.

As they walked, Tim, Thomas, and Leo covered their noses with the tops of their shirts, pressing their hands against their faces. The smell was overwhelming, a sickeningly sweet brew of citrus,

**Student volunteers from the St. Charles Seminary carry a coffin for burial at Holy Cross Cemetery, October 1918.**

fish, and licorice. Tim halted and held his hand over his mouth, stifling the urge to vomit. The threesome hurried to join the others.

The volunteers gripped paper and pencils to record where each body was buried, in hopes that the graves could be more easily found by relatives later on. The young men separated into groups of three and began digging individual graves. They then carried the decomposing corpses to their final resting places.

At Tim's insistence, after every burial each threesome would stand over the grave, and one student would say a prayer. Then, after scratching a name in their notepad, they would pile a few shovelfuls of dirt onto the body and move on to create the next sad grave.

Over the next few hours, the group of thirty-five young men buried sixty-two bodies as the sun set on the tranquil cemetery grounds. At 8:00 p.m., under a moonlit sky, Tim, Thomas, and Leo performed the last burial ceremony of the day. Tim and Leo put down their shovels as Thomas patted down the last bit of dirt with his. The young men then joined hands over the grave.

It was Leo's turn to pray: "Out of the depths I have cried to thee, O Lord: Lord, hear my voice . . ."

As Leo spoke, the other volunteers, having already packed up for the day, gathered around the grave with heads bowed.

At last, the first gruesome day of laying Philadelphia's dead to rest was over. Before joining the rest of his team on the walk to the train station, Tim wrote the name of the last person on his master list: Sylvia Epp.

———————

"Sister. Sister, please, some water," a voice said in an overcrowded sickroom at Emergency Hospital No. 8. Sister Katherine looked up from the bruise-colored woman she was tending, who lay in a bed smeared with yellow and red stains.

"Sister, where am I?" another voice croaked.

"Sister, ice," hissed another, weakly.

"Sister, milk," another near her murmured.

"Just a moment," Sister Katherine said through her mask to the man lying in a bed nearby. "I'm checking on Miss Claire." She turned back to her patient, a young woman of sixteen who stared at the ceiling with milky eyes as if she were in a deep reverie, listening to music that no one else could hear. Her mother and sister lay dead in their beds a few rows over, though Sister Katherine hadn't had the heart to tell her. In the beds next to Claire lay her three nieces, whose father, grandmother, and aunt had just expired from the illness. Claire was all they had now. And they were all she had. But she hadn't spoken in hours, and watching the young woman as she twitched, Sister Katherine felt sure that she would meet her maker soon. Sister Katherine closed her eyes and began to quietly recite the last rites, when all of a sudden Claire gripped the nun's hand tightly with her bony, sticky fingers. Startled, Sister Katherine looked at Claire, whose cloudy eyeballs were moving around once again.

"Sister," she said through her cracked lips.

"Yes, Miss Claire, I'm right here."

"Where . . . where am I?"

"Emergency Hospital, love," Sister Katherine said softly.

Claire blinked slowly.

"But . . . how can that be? The sisters are here."

"Yes." Sister Katherine smiled, looking around the room at the other volunteer nuns from St. Charles who were helping the ill. "We're here."

Suddenly Claire squeezed Sister Katherine's arm with renewed vigor, clinging to the nun's arm as if it were the only thing keeping her from slipping out of the land of the living.

"Sister," she sighed, pointing a finger at the ceiling. "Do you see the angels?"

Sister Katherine looked up. No angels, just a flickering light fixture. But then she looked over at Claire's nieces.

"Yes, love." Sister Katherine nodded. "I see them."

A sudden howl of pain from the ward across the hall split the air. Sister Katherine looked up—it sounded like William, the older man whom the staff had had to restrain earlier. The last time she saw him he was strapped to his bed and squirming. Sister Katherine moved to get up, but Claire held her arm.

"Oh, but now they're gone!" Claire said breathlessly, still clinging to Sister Katherine with one hand. "Where'd they go, Sister? You saw them, didn't you?"

"Yes, my dear," Sister Katherine said. "The angels are sleeping now. You should sleep, too."

Claire inhaled slowly, sounding like sandpaper being rubbed against rusty metal. There was no exhale. Sister Katherine gazed at the young woman's face—her irises, already barely visible in the cloudy white of her eyes, seemed to have rolled back into her sockets.

"The angels are . . ." Claire's grip on Katherine's arm began to loosen.

Sister Katherine placed her hand under Claire's nose and felt for breath. There was none. She turned to the young nieces. Were they still alive? She felt she couldn't tell the living from the dead anymore. She rose and stepped out to the hallway, following the sound of William's wailing. Padding into the men's ward, she saw him in the first row of beds, struggling against the straps that held him down.

"Now, William, what's the matter, mister?" Rachel said, coming out of the office. "You still trying to catch the kaiser?" She stood over William as he wriggled and writhed, screaming and yelping powerlessly. Sister Katherine was soon by her side and gazing over William as he struggled against the restraints. Blood oozed out of every part of his body: out of his eye sockets, ears, mouth, fingernails, and toenails, and through the sores on his legs and arms. Sister Katherine gasped and closed her eyes, silently begging God to show him some measure of mercy.

Suddenly William stopped screaming. "Somebody tryin' to kill me," he growled in a low voice. Then he lay perfectly still and closed his eyes.

Sister Katherine wiped tears from her eyes and looked at Rachel, who was fearlessly kneeling down beside him.

"William, no one is trying to hurt you. Sister Katherine and I just want to help."

William moved his jaw slowly from side to side. He opened his eyes and saw Sister Katherine standing above him.

"Is that my Lil?"

Sister Katherine looked at Rachel, who shrugged her shoulders. She stood up and leaned in to whisper in Sister Katherine's ear.

"I'd just say yes," Rachel said. "It'll keep him sweet."

Sister Katherine looked down at William and nodded hesitantly.

"Yes, that's her," William said. Though the restraints crossed twice over his chest, he was able to move his forearms toward

Sister Katherine. She knelt down and placed one of her hands in his.

"Yeah, that's my Lil," he said. He closed his eyes.

———

Harry, Harriet, and Barium sat on the wooden floor of Aunt Selma and Uncle Mike's apartment, browsing through the penny candy they had bought at the drugstore. Harry panned for jelly beans as he chewed on a Tootsie Roll, and Harriet and Barium shared a small bag of Hershey's Kisses. Uncle Mike was on the phone, speaking to someone in a hushed tone so that the Milani children wouldn't hear. After a few minutes he hung up and sat down at the table. Aunt Selma set a pot of soup on it, then looked over at Barium and nodded.

"Hey, Harry," Barium said, "save some of the candy for later, huh? Let's have some dinner. You wanna?"

Harry looked at his sister. Harriet furrowed her brow and turned to Barium. "Are you sure it's okay?" she asked him. "I can make us some dinner at our place if Mommy's still sleeping."

"Oh, sure." Barium smiled. "It was Aunt Selma's idea to have you stay."

Harry and Harriet looked at Aunt Selma for confirmation. She nodded, trying to force a smile.

"You kids can stay as long as you like," Uncle Mike said.

"You could even spend the night," Barium agreed. "Couldn't they, Auntie?"

"Yes, of course," Aunt Selma said. "We could make up a bed of blankets on the floor for you."

Harriet nodded hesitantly. "Won't our mother wonder where we are?"

"Oh . . ." Selma glanced worriedly at her nephew. "Well, Barium could . . . let her know where you are, couldn't you, Barium?"

Barium nodded slowly but kept his eyes fixed on the wall.

"Anyway," Uncle Mike stood and gestured to the children to come sit at the table. "She's probably too tired to cook. Why don't you kids come have some supper?"

They gathered around the rectangular wooden table as Aunt Selma laid out bowls and spoons.

"Maybe we can take some back to Mommy and Daddy?" Harry whispered to his sister. She elbowed him lightly in the arm.

"See how you like it," Aunt Selma said as she ladled soup into Harry's bowl. "I just threw it together quickly with a little celery and garlic."

Uncle Mike, Barium, and Harriet hungrily started spooning soup into their mouths. Harry sat in his chair and placed the rest of his uneaten Tootsie Roll on the table beside his bowl. Harriet snatched it up quickly and put it in the napkin on her lap, shooting her brother a scolding look. Harry looked at his steaming bowl of soup, then back at Harriet.

"Harry, eat your soup," she said.

Harry swirled his spoon around in the bowl, then lifted it to his mouth. He blew on the spoon, touched his tongue to the spoon briefly, then lowered it once again to the bowl. Harriet shook her head at him, then turned to Aunt Selma.

"It's really good, Mrs. . . . ." Harriet realized she didn't know what to call her.

"Oh, sweetie, just call me Aunt Selma."

Harriet smiled. "Thank you for the soup, Aunt Selma. It's really good."

But Harry pushed his bowl away.

"Harry!" his sister scolded.

"Did that Tootsie Roll spoil your appetite?" Aunt Selma smiled.

Barium looked at Harry. "You okay, buddy?"

"Yeah," Harry said, his mouth barely moving. "Just not very hungry."

Barium put his hand on Harry's head and mussed his hair, then looked over at Harriet, who was happily sipping her soup. He wondered how on earth he was going to tell them about their parents. The longer he put it off, the harder it would be. He had made his aunt and uncle promise to let him do it. But would he be able to?

Harry stood up from the table and wiped his brow.

"Aunt Selma," he said, "can I go lie down?"

———— ◆ ————

The seminary students rode the train from Holy Cross Cemetery back to St. Charles in silence. Some slept on the shoulders of their seatmates; some stared out the window at the moonlit foliage zooming by in a blur; others sat with their heads against the backs of their seats, eyes glassy and half-closed. All were exhausted, covered in mud and sweat, and overwhelmed by the horrific sights and smells they'd encountered while burying the bodies.

Tim sat in the middle of the train compartment, flipping through his notebook where he'd written the names of the dead. Next to him, Leo slumped against the window, his head pressing on the glass and his shoulders slowly rising and falling in his exhausted slumber. Across the aisle, in a seat by himself, Thomas sat silently, eyes closed and head bowed as if for prayer. He suddenly opened his eyes and gasped.

Tim dropped his notebook and hopped out of his seat. The other students on the train turned their heads.

"Thomas, what's wrong?"

Thomas looked around, rediscovering where he was. He shuddered.

"Oh, sorry," he mumbled. "I was having a bad dream."

Tim knelt down beside his friend as some of the other students whispered among themselves.

"Do you want to tell me what you saw in your dream?"

Thomas stared straight ahead. "I was burying a little girl," he began. "Three years old, maybe. She had on a pink flowery dress and white stockings. I looked at her bluish face and couldn't stop myself from giving it a little kiss. But, Tim, when I raised my head up, her face . . . it was disintegrating. The skin all over her body was disappearing. And the dress and stockings. After a few moments all that was left was a bloody skeleton. It was like she was melting in my arms."

"Is that when you woke up?" Tim asked.

"No." Thomas just shook his head slowly. Finally he looked over at Tim. "I couldn't bury her. I placed her in the ground and tried to cover her with dirt, but the dirt just slid off of her. Just fell right off. I shoveled faster and harder, but still her blood-red skull was still there, looking up at me. That's when I woke up."

Thomas was out of breath, as if he'd just slumped into his seat after competing in a race.

"You're going to be all right, Thomas," Tim reassured his friend. "We're seeing things we never thought we'd see. The Lord is testing us . . . but you know he wouldn't put a challenge in front of us that he didn't think we could rise to. Just remember that, okay?"

Thomas wiped the tears that had sprung from his eyes.

"Because we have to come back tomorrow and do the same thing. We've got to steel ourselves for it. There's no other way."

Thomas inhaled, wiped more tears, and nodded.

"We were put here by the Almighty," Tim continued, "to help usher these poor souls into the heavenly kingdom." As he spoke Tim couldn't stop his own eyes from misting over. He patted Thomas on the leg and returned to his seat. Looking over at Leo, still slumped against the window, Tim chuckled.

"Well, you woke up everyone but old Leo." He smiled.

Thomas gazed over at Leo from across the aisle. "He's dead to the world."

Tim frowned at this and leaned in toward Leo. "Leo? You okay?" Leo didn't move. "Leo?" Tim tapped his friend on the shoulder, then grabbed Leo's shoulder and shook it. "Leo?"

Leo suddenly gasped and jerked around. There was blood seeping from his nose and ears.

Tim leaped up in shock and backed into the aisle, and Leo plummeted face-first onto Tim's now-empty seat.

# TO THE DEADHOUSE

WILMER KRUSEN SAT ON A bench outside the mayor's office at city hall in the early morning, flipping through a stack of papers while he waited for Mayor Smith to arrive. He'd had only a few hours of sleep again last night, overwhelmed as he was with emergency hospital visits, meetings with city officials and Red Cross representatives, trips to cemeteries and funeral homes, and even filling in as emergency medical personnel at hospitals with a few volunteer nuns and nurses but no doctors. He looked at a memo clipped to the stack of papers in his lap, on which he'd scribbled the latest available numbers:

*October 9*

*4,166 new cases*

*428 deaths*

Wilmer rubbed his eyes and sighed. He'd seen so much death in the past week—bodies lying on the ground, on porches, in alleyways; slumped in chairs, against walls or on kitchen tables; and stacked on trucks and wagons or outside funeral homes, hospitals, and cemeteries. Each of them struck Wilmer as a sad

**Red Cross nurses—such as these in St. Louis, Missouri—played a vital role in fighting the epidemic.**

failure of medicine, the field he'd dedicated his life to. When he was a student, the field of medicine seemed like an exciting frontier, producing a new miracle every day. He was later drawn to the public health sphere, feeling that that was where he could have the most positive impact. But now here he was, facing the biggest public health crisis in the city's history, and he was utterly defenseless against a quick-moving epidemic that would burn itself out when it was good and ready, and not a minute before, no matter what he did.

Though Wilmer had never been a religious man, he found himself envying the nuns at the emergency hospitals across Philadelphia, and the faith that bolstered them. He didn't know if God existed, but he'd always believed that medical science could be depended on to provide answers and save lives. Philadelphia's dead were proving him tragically wrong.

It was only when he was alone, during quiet moments when he wasn't being pulled this way and that, that the enormity of the devastation began to crystallize in his mind. It was only at times like this, when no one else was around, that he allowed himself to grieve the loss of his fellow Philadelphians. Placing the papers on the bench beside him, he looked around him, then surrendered his head into his hands and wept.

The mayor's office door opened with a frantic rattle, and Mayor Smith stepped out. He looked disheveled, the ring of curly white hair around his head reaching wildly skyward.

"What is it, Krusen?"

"Oh, Mayor Smith, I didn't know you were in." Wilmer shot to his feet, nervously wiping his eyes.

"Been here all night. Posted bond yesterday, and just wanted to lay low for a spell."

Wilmer had been so busy with his health commissioner duties that he'd forgotten about the mayor's indictment for corruption. Not being a part of the mayor's inner circle—a circle known for staying in power while getting rich in the process—he wouldn't have been involved in the damage-control effort, even without the health catastrophe he had on his hands.

They walked into the office, where the mayor had made a bed of the leather couch and a blanket of his winter coat. The mayor stumbled past the couch to his desk and sat down while Wilmer followed behind him.

"Please, Krusen, sit."

Wilmer looked around, wondering where to sit—the two chairs that were usually placed before the mayor's desk were overturned and lying on the floor. Wilmer assumed that, after his court hearing, the mayor had taken out his anger, frustration, or drunkenness—or a mixture of all three—on his office furniture.

"I'll just stand," Wilmer said. "This'll only take a minute."

"Well, that's about all I can give you. What is it?"

"I wonder if we might be able to arrange a thorough cleaning of the streets in the southern neighborhoods—"

"Street cleaning? Don't you have better things to worry about? I've seen the bodies stacking up . . ."

"Yes, sir," Wilmer replied, trying to remain calm, "and I've managed to organize more teams of volunteers to collect and transport the bodies to the cemeteries."

"And?"

"The fact remains, the streets on the south side are in a ghastly condition. They were before this flu hit, and now they're even worse. They're filthy. And filth breeds disease. We've already got a ravenous sickness on our hands; we don't need to give it any more help. I think if we could clean them up a bit, we might slow this thing down."

"I've already given you all the money the city's got, Krusen."

"No, sir, I'm not asking for money." Wilmer looked Mayor Smith directly in the eyes. "Not for me."

"Well, who's asking for money then, Doctor?"

Wilmer sighed.

"I need men," he said. "Some of your men. To come clean the streets. They've got the trucks, the tools, the manpower. And you've got . . . your skills of persuasion."

"My what?" The mayor laughed. "What are you saying?"

"We both know that you've engaged in some . . . *creative* accounting in the past, Mayor Smith. I'd hazard a guess that there is money that is not on the official books that you could put to use."

"Now just hold on a second, Krusen," the mayor spat. "I don't know who you think you are coming in here trying to—"

"There were 428 deaths yesterday." Wilmer raised his voice to his boss for the first time ever. Something about seeing the mayor so disheveled—still dressed in the suit he wore the day before, his hair wiry and wild like a dried mop—gave Wilmer a surge of resolve to bend the old liar to his will. "And 4,166 new cases."

The mayor glared at Wilmer, unaccustomed to being addressed this way.

"And those are just the ones we know about," Wilmer continued. "The ones that have been reported. There are certainly plenty of Philadelphians who have simply dropped dead in their houses—whole families, likely. Multiply those numbers I gave you by about five if you want a prediction of the real number who'll die before this whole thing is over."

The mayor sat speechless.

"You should have canceled that parade," Wilmer said. "You could have, you should have. But you didn't. So you need to do everything in your power now to address this tragedy, a tragedy you helped create."

Wilmer looked down at his papers—the numbers he'd scribbled, the frantic requests for more medicine, more staff, and more linens. He stood up. "I'll assume you can make that requested arrangement, Mr. Mayor," he said. "And I thank you."

Without another look, Wilmer turned and walked out.

Rushing down the hall, he couldn't help but flush with embarrassment at this sad little triumph. Forcing a city's mayor to have the streets cleaned wouldn't normally count as an amazing show of strength. But right now Wilmer would take what he could get.

———

Kneeling by Leo's bed, Tim wiped the crusted blood off his friend's nose and upper lip with a wet cloth. Leo inhaled deeply, the phlegm rattling in his throat sounding like a pile of rocks being scraped together.

Leo's breathing had deteriorated ever since they'd arrived at the infirmary. As soon as the train had arrived at the station in Lower Merion Township, Tim called a car to take himself, Thomas, and a half-conscious Leo to the infirmary at St. Charles. Tim and Thomas had carried Leo inside and had taken turns all night sitting by his bed as he slept. Tim wondered if Leo was Lower Merion's first influenza patient. It was early morning now, and they would be leaving for the cemetery soon.

More blood trickled out of Leo's nostrils, and Tim wiped it away. He thought he could see a faint blue tint to his friend's face, which was wet with perspiration. Maybe it was the dim light in the room. He tried not to think about the multitude of dark blue bodies he'd helped bury the day before. He heard the creak of a door opening and turned to see a nun approaching with a tray. Sister Margaret was the only nurse on staff at the infirmary, all the others having been called away to help in emergency hospitals in Philadelphia.

"I've brought some cold cloths for his face," she said. "And some Vicks that we might rub on his chest."

"Thank you, Sister." Tim took one of the rolled-up red cloths from the tray and pressed it to Leo's forehead.

"If he wakes, I've got some tea ready for him. It will do his system good."

Leo rolled his head around on his wet pillow, maybe feeling for a dry patch, and the cloth rolled off. Catching it, Tim waited for Leo to settle again, then replaced the cloth on his forehead.

Leo opened his eyes.

"Leo?" Tim blurted out. "Can you hear me?"

Leo slowly closed his eyes, then opened them again and looked straight at Tim. He opened his mouth to speak, but the rocks started scraping again, and he surrendered to a coughing fit. A knock sounded at the door, and Thomas poked his head in.

"How's he doing?"

"Not good," Tim said.

"I'll check back on you boys in a little while." Sister Margaret padded to the door, holding it open for Thomas to enter.

"Do you want to take a break?" Thomas asked Tim as he stepped into the room. "Maybe go get some fresh air?"

*Fresh air,* Tim thought. With all the death and sickness surrounding him, it seemed like an eternity since he'd breathed fresh air. Did it even exist?

"Yeah," Tim answered. "I think I'll go to the chapel, say a few prayers."

Thomas looked at Tim and sighed. "What's the use?" he mumbled.

"The use? Of prayer? Strange question for a theology student."

"I don't know." Thomas shook his head. "It just seems . . . all those dead bodies. Dead children. Dead families. Do you think they prayed?"

Tim thought for a moment. "I imagine many of them did."

"And did God hear their prayers?"

"Of course He did."

"Then why?" Thomas sounded angry. "Why didn't He answer them? Why are they all in the ground now?"

"We can't understand the mysteries of God's divine plan, Thomas."

Thomas scowled.

"But I do know this," Tim said, putting his hand on Thomas's shoulder. "We are here for a reason. I mean you and me. We were put here to help. To release people from their earthly burdens. And"—he looked at Leo—"right now, we are here to take care of our friend."

Thomas looked at Tim, then at Leo.

"It's all we can do," Tim said. He went to the door and looked at his watch. "I'll be back in an hour or so, and then we'll meet the others at the train station." The door creaked again as he strode out.

Thomas sat down in the chair next to the bed, placing his head in his hand. Leo coughed again, and Thomas noticed that he was bleeding from the nose. He grabbed a cloth and wiped the blood away. As he did this Leo turned his head and exhaled deeply, the rocks rattling in his throat. A look of anguish overtook Thomas's face as he gazed at his friend.

Blood trickled out of Leo's ear and onto the pillow.

———

"Excuse me, Sister," Rachel whispered, "we've got to clear space. Time to bring folks out to the deadhouse. Can we take this poor girl?"

Sister Katherine finished praying over the corpse of a young woman and raised her bowed head.

"Yes, indeed, Nurse Rachel. She's gone."

Sister Katherine moved away from the bed, and a burly orderly appeared to lift the girl and carry her out.

Sister Katherine moved among the beds in the large open room, carrying a tray loaded with cups of water and ice. She was in the women's acute ward—a ninety-bed hall reserved for those who weren't expected to live through the day. No lights were on in the large room, but the sun shone through the many high windows, casting thick stripes of light along the floor. Every cot was occupied, and ninety women filled the air with their moans, howls, and coughs. Cries for water, a doctor, a priest, or ice chips reached her ears every few seconds.

Sister Katherine stopped at the bed of a young mother. The woman's face was dark blue, and her lips were cracked and bloody. She was barely conscious, though her eyes were wide open. Her little girl and one-year-old boy lay on the cot next to her. Sister Katherine placed the tray on a counter, took a cup of water from it, and plucked a cotton ball from a glass container. She dipped the cotton ball in the water, knelt down, and slid it along the woman's lips. The woman moaned faintly with gratitude, though she couldn't form words.

Sister Katherine went about her work with grim determination. With so many patients to tend, so many entreaties to answer, so much suffering to try to alleviate, she'd had no time to dwell on the horror she'd witnessed day in, day out: the dead bodies sticking to the bedsheets; the awful screams and pathetic whimpers of the dying; husbands cradling their dying wives; mothers watching their babies slip away. Keeping a constant prayer on her lips, if only to repeat to herself, Sister Katherine performed her duties for each patient with care and gentleness and then moved on to the next one, all the while trying to ignore the questions in the back of her mind. Why was this happening? Why to some people and not to others? She'd been living and walking among the sick for a few days now, and yet she'd not exhibited the slightest symptom of illness. Was this a sign that her purpose was to usher the dying into their heavenly paradise? If that was what she was being called to do, she accepted it, but . . . why her? And these poor people . . . why must they die? And so terribly. . . .

She gazed over at the baby boy and felt her heart sink. Blood covered his nose and mouth. Sister Katherine hurried over to the cot and felt his arm for a pulse: there was none. She closed her eyes and breathed a quiet prayer, then, unable to bring herself to look at him again, she wrapped the sheets around him and cradled him in her arms. She would take him out herself—she couldn't bear the thought of handing him to an orderly and just returning to her patients. She hugged the swaddled baby to her chest.

Suddenly the double doors opened, and Rachel walked into the ward with a young man wearing a white physician's coat.

"Sister Katherine, this is Dr. Lawrence. He's a resident physician and will be helping—" She saw the bloody bundle in Sister Katherine's arms and stopped talking.

"Thank you so much for coming to help us," Sister Katherine said, her eyes filled with tears. "May the Lord bless you and keep you as you work." She walked on.

"Thank you, Sister," Dr. Lawrence said, mesmerized by the look of anguished grace on the nun's face.

Sister Katherine left the ward in silence.

"Where's she going?" the young doctor asked Rachel, as Sister Katherine walked out the doors.

"To the deadhouse, Dr. Lawrence."

---

"Harry?" Barium whispered as he stooped over the cot where Harry was sleeping. He'd just come in to check on Harry, who'd gone to bed immediately after supper last night and slept straight through to the morning.

"Harry!" But Harry didn't answer. Barium nudged Harry on the shoulder lightly and felt heat radiating from the boy's body. Still Harry slept. His chest rose and fell with his raspy breathing. Barium had heard that sound before. He shoved the thought out of his head and backed out of the room.

"Is he okay?" Harriet asked Barium as he closed the bedroom door.

"He's still asleep. I tried to wake him, but he's sleeping very deeply."

Aunt Selma came in the front door with a paper bag in her hand. "I got some aspirin. Did you get him to drink some of that whiskey?"

"No," Barium said. "I couldn't get him to wake up. He's really sawing a log."

"Well, we should try to wake him up in a little bit. Until then, hopefully that Vicks and camphor are helping. I'll warm up some soup for him."

"Where's your uncle Mike?" Harriet asked Barium.

"He's . . ." Barium looked at his aunt.

"He's helping some neighbors do something," she said, walking to the tiny kitchen.

"Did you check on my parents?" Harriet looked at Aunt Selma pleadingly. "You said you'd stop by on your way to the store. Did you see them?"

Aunt Selma opened her mouth to respond, but Barium interrupted. "Harriet . . ." He gestured for her to sit beside him on the tattered sofa. "There's something that we need to tell you." Barium saw that Harriet's eyes had quickly filled with tears. Did she already know?

"You know about this flu—it's taken . . . many people," Barium said. Harriet nodded and wiped her eyes, her lips trembling.

"I'm afraid that . . . it's taken them, too."

Aunt Selma left the stove and hurried over to sit next to Harriet. Harriet folded into Aunt Selma's arms and sobbed.

"Darling, I'm so sorry. So, so sorry. Barry just lost his mother, and I lost my sister, too. We're going to help you get through this. You're in a safe place here, and you can stay."

Suddenly Harriet jerked her head up as if she'd just received an electric shock. "What about Harry?"

Aunt Selma paused. "He's just resting. And we're going to take care of him. I'll go check on him now, give him some aspirin." Aunt Selma stood, walked the few steps to the bedroom, and went in. Barium and Harriet heard her whisper something to Harry and, after a few moments, heard him answer softly. Harriet lowered her head into her hands.

Barium placed his hand on Harriet's back and stroked it slowly as she sobbed.

"Can I go see them?" she said, her face still covered by her palms. "At the apartment?" Barium was silent, and Harriet raised her head to look him in the eye. "I want to see them."

"Harriet, it's not safe for you to go over there," Barium said. "You don't want to risk touching anything or—"

Harriet jumped up and scurried out the apartment door.

"Harriet!" Barium followed her down the stairs and out to the street. But she had already halted, just outside the main door. She stared at a wagon in the street, full of corpses. There was Uncle Mike, along with a few other men from the neighborhood, loading two more into the back. Slowly she stepped toward the wagon, staring directly at the bodies. Uncle Mike saw her approaching, whispered to the other men to back away, and yelled at the driver of the wagon to move along.

Harriet stepped into the street as the wagon pulled away. A breeze lifted up the sheets covering the bodies. Suddenly she saw a lock of long brown hair and a strand of blue ribbon billowing out as the wagon lumbered down the bumpy road. The hair was the same brown as hers. That ribbon was her mother's.

# DEEPLY CYANOTIC

At Holy Cross Cemetery Thomas stabbed the ground with his shovel, sweating from the exertion. It was mid-morning, and he and fifteen of the other volunteers from the seminary, all clad in their medical masks, had been digging a large pit for a few hours now. The bodies were piling up—more arriving every hour—and needed to be speedily interred in a common grave. The open trench was already about ten feet across and twelve feet deep, and on the opposite side was Tim, bent over and lifting a shovelful of dirt out of the ground, his face and medical mask streaked with mud.

Thomas looked up from his shovel at the vaults and sheds nearby, overflowing with makeshift coffins, and at the wagons and trucks stacked high with bodies for burial, stretching in a long row by the cemetery gates. Fresh graves were being opened up everywhere, in every direction. The cemetery resembled a battlefield torn up by shells and littered with corpses. A steady procession of vehicles pressed at the gates—trucks, coal carts, ash wagons—all conveying more bodies. Undertakers had run out of caskets, and their substitutes peppered the grounds; there were bodies in homemade rough boxes, soap boxes, orange crates, coarse burlap bags. Overwhelmed, Thomas began to tremble slightly. He rubbed his eyes and placed his hands on the shovel

**Students from the St. Charles Seminary dig mass graves in the Holy Cross Cemetery, Philadelphia.**

handle. He felt like he would be burying bodies for eternity. There was no end to this gruesome job.

But even amid the stench of death that was closing in like the dark clouds of a gathering storm, something was even more troubling: he couldn't get his last glimpse of Leo's face out of his mind. When he'd realized his friend was bleeding from the ears, he had propped up Leo's head and pressed a cloth to the side of his head. The blood had clotted a few minutes later and had stopped flowing, but Leo hadn't come back to consciousness before Thomas had had to leave him to the care of Sister Margaret and join Tim and the rest of the volunteers to make the trek back out to Holy Cross. The flu victims surrounding him felt like harbingers of what was in store for poor Leo. Many of the corpses Thomas saw on the ground had sizable scabs on the ears.

"He'll be back soon," Thomas said to himself, not realizing he was speaking out loud.

"What's that?" Tim asked.

Thomas looked up. "Oh, nothing. I just . . . thought I saw someone I recognized over there on the ground." He lifted up his shovel and thrust it into the ground again.

Tim nodded, looking warily at his friend. Thomas hadn't spoken the whole way to the cemetery, except to say that Leo still hadn't woken up. Another full day of burials, of wading through the pungent reek of decomposition to fetch more victims, of dealing with the repulsiveness of the bodies themselves, some of which were so corroded that the skin was slipping off them like wet tissue paper—it might be more than Thomas could take.

Tim had to admit that he was struggling, too. He'd never once doubted that he'd been called to live a life of godly service—he'd never considered another career. And for the past few days he'd tried to be a good Christian soldier, single-mindedly applying himself to the task at hand without question. But, replaying over and over in his head his recent conversation with Thomas in Leo's sickroom, he couldn't shake a sense of disappointment at the answers he'd given Thomas about the power—the necessity—of prayer. He'd tried to kick aside his friend's doubts, but he couldn't ignore how flat his reassurances had fallen.

Thomas had scowled at Tim's assertions that God *did* hear the prayers of the dying, that it was impossible to know God's plan but that they should be assured that there *was* one. But looking around himself now, at the endless cavalcade of horrific, grotesque, and, yes, *cruel* death, Tim couldn't blame Thomas for scowling. There on the ground was a boy of no more than ten, stiff, lifeless, horror-stricken. And was that his mother next to him, in a muddy nightgown, her jaw locked open as if issuing a howl from the grave? He gazed over at the seminarians in the trench, laying decomposing bodies end to end to end. And over at the cemetery entrance, another collection of wagons pulled up, piled high with more carcasses.

It all seemed to mock Tim's claims that God had a plan. This wasn't a plan—this was chaos.

Tim looked around for Monsignor Drumgoole. The monsignor had ridden with the seminarians out to Holy Cross that morning so he could get an idea of the number of volunteers that would need to stay on-site in the coming days. On the train he'd mentioned there were other local places in need that had been putting in calls to St. Charles, desperately looking for help.

"I'm reluctant to give up any of you boys," the monsignor had said. "After all, it won't be easy to find volunteers to handle bodies and coffins all day, and it's well-nigh impossible to find hired hands willing to brave the pestilence. But we may be able to spare a few of you where the need is greatest."

Tim grasped at this idea like a life raft. Anything had to be better than this.

"Have you seen Monsignor Drumgoole?" Tim asked Thomas, who shook his head without looking up. Suddenly they heard a commotion at the entrance. A family had gathered at the gate and was talking to Monsignor Drumgoole. The father was holding a small shoebox and raising his voice in a loud whimper. The monsignor nodded his head and put his hand on the man's shoulder. The father moaned and held the shoebox above his head as his wife and two young daughters huddled and cried.

Stepping away, the father darted into the cemetery and saw Tim looking his way. Yelling out in Italian, the man rushed over to Tim, firing off a series of impenetrable questions and gesturing around at the bodies and back at the shoebox he held. Tim looked at the box in the man's arms and hoped that he didn't know what was in it. Without warning, the man pulled the top of it off to reveal a tiny baby, dead from the flu. The box was its casket.

*"Mio dio!"* the man cried out, raising the box into the air with both hands. *"Perché mi hai abbandonato?"*

A cold shiver shooting down his spine, Tim gazed over at Thomas, who was staring at the box and shaking his head, as if to convince himself that it contained only shoes.

"Lord, help me get him out of here," Tim prayed.

More people pushed through the gate to enter the cemetery. A young girl nudged her way through the small crowd until she stood in front of Monsignor Drumgoole. She looked past him to a wagon that had just arrived and was parked a few yards away on the cemetery lawn. She haltingly started to move toward it.

"Harriet!" a voice called from a few yards away. Harriet stopped in her tracks and turned to see Barium dashing up the road. He tore through the people gathered at the entrance and galloped up to her.

"Wow," Barium said, putting his hands on his hips and bending at the waist to catch his breath. "You are *fast*."

---

"Most of them are deeply cyanotic, with escalated respiration and nasal hemorrhaging," Dr. Lawrence said to Sister Katherine, closing and locking the ward door behind him after completing a quick sweep of the acute ward to look at the state of the patients. He wiped his brow and ran his hand through his neatly slicked-back hair, sending a pencil he'd placed behind his ear to the floor. "It's central and peripheral—all over their bodies," he continued as he bent to pick up the pencil. "A number are so far gone they already look dead, though they're still breathing. Many are delirious and a few are . . . active."

Sister Katherine furrowed her brow, not having understood much of what she had just heard.

"Forgive me, Doctor . . . what does *cyanotic* mean?"

"Oh, I'm sorry, Sister," Dr. Lawrence said, trying to manage a smile despite feeling thoroughly spooked. "I've been in school for too long."

"You're doing wonderfully, Doctor," Sister Katherine said.

"Well, *cyanotic* is just a fancy word for the blue and purple discoloration of the skin. It's due to the lack of oxygen in the

**A nurse outside influenza medical tents, September 13, 1918, location unknown**

tissues." Dr. Lawrence hoped that Sister Katherine couldn't tell how terrified he was of what he was seeing. He was a student doctor and had never even been left in charge of more than a few patients at a time, much less an entire shift at an understaffed emergency hospital heaving with dying patients. And these patients—they were, to a person, indescribably ghoulish—like the walking dead out of some fantastical medieval legend.

"And when you say *active*, you mean . . ." Sister Katherine waited for him to interrupt, but Dr. Lawrence just stared at the floor, thinking of what to say. After an awkward silence, he shrugged and unlocked the ward door.

Inside the wide-open room, a chilling symphony of moans, cries, and screams filled the air. One patient who was strapped to her cot shook maniacally, her hands gripped the sides of her bed, rattling them as if they were the bars of a cage. An orderly was doing battle with a large, two-hundred-pound woman, taking her by the arms and forcing her back to her cot. She writhed and screamed, flailing and biting like a wild animal. Dr. Lawrence rushed over to help, and the two men managed to strap her to her bed, but the straps couldn't keep her from reaching up with her forearms and tearing at her curly brown locks, ripping them out in fistfuls and hurling them to the floor. Nearby, another woman sat on her cot, tearing at her nightgown and trying to rip it from her body. When the woman spotted Sister Katherine, she screamed for water. This scream was followed by another scream from another corner of the ward. And then another. And another. A raspy chorus of women shrieked for water, for ice, for air, and even for death. Sister Katherine stepped through the ward, screams echoing all around her. All the patients were so discolored that she couldn't tell if they were black or white.

"Water! Do you hear me? I need water!"

Sister Katherine ducked over to the sink, where the trays and cups were stacked. Hands shaking, she filled a pitcher with water and had begun pouring it into the cups when suddenly Rachel began shouting.

"Sister, please! Over here! I need help!"

Rachel stood behind a patient, holding her down by the shoulders. The woman was a deep purple, and her skin was wet with pus and sweat. She writhed under Rachel's grip and flailed her arms, attempting to give the nurse a smack.

Sister Katherine put down the pitcher and scurried over to Rachel.

"Sister, this is Bonnie. It's okay, Bonnie, we just need to strap you back in." To Sister Katherine, Rachel whispered, "She broke free somehow. Hold her down while I go get the restraints."

Sister Katherine took Rachel's place and held Bonnie down. "Please hurry," she said. "I'm not very strong."

Rachel looked over at Dr. Lawrence, who was still trying to stabilize the large woman a few rows over. "Okay, just hold tight. I won't be a second," she said as she bolted over to the cupboards along the wall. She scoured them for anything she could use to tie Bonnie down.

Bonnie continued squirming, bellowing nonsensical sounds that echoed through the cavernous room. Then suddenly she stopped moving and sat perfectly silent. Sister Katherine reflexively loosened her grip on Bonnie's shoulders just slightly, not wanting to hurt her. Bonnie turned to Katherine and spat in her face. As Katherine reared back in shock, Bonnie leaped up off the cot and bounded toward Rachel.

"Nurse Rachel!" Sister Katherine shouted.

Rachel turned around and broke Bonnie's surge with her outstretched arms. She held on tightly as the woman tried to wriggle free.

Dr. Lawrence rushed over and grabbed Bonnie from behind, pulling her back toward her bed. Rachel followed with another set of white straps, quickly fastening them to the underside of the cot while Bonnie writhed and wailed against Dr. Lawrence. Before Rachel could secure the straps, Bonnie broke free again and dashed away, right into the path of Sister Katherine, who stood before her with a full glass pitcher of water. Sister Katherine quickly whispered, "Forgive me," and swung the pitcher forward, dousing Bonnie in the face. Bonnie shrieked, grabbed the pitcher from Sister Katherine, and brought it down on the nun's head.

As Katherine fell, a spray of blood flecked the white tiled floor.

---

Aunt Selma stroked Harry's back as he groaned.

"It's okay, honey, it's okay," she whispered. Harry vomited up the soup into the pan that Uncle Mike was holding, then continued to groan as he dry-heaved. When he was finished, he collapsed back onto the pillow, his face damp with sweat and red from exertion. Aunt Selma placed her hand on his forehead—he was burning hot. Uncle Mike took the pan out to the sink in the kitchenette.

"Honey, can you hear me?" Aunt Selma said, leaning down so her face was close to Harry's. Harry opened his eyes.

"Mommy?"

Aunt Selma raised her eyebrows.

"Yes, Mommy," Harry mumbled, his eyelids narrowed, the eyes beneath them glazed. "Can you get me some water?"

Aunt Selma nodded. "Of course I can, sweetie. I'll be right back."

"Okay." Harry turned on his side and closed his eyes.

As Uncle Mike finished washing out the pan, Aunt Selma joined him at the sink. Harry had started coughing—it was a deep cough, erupting from his chest and pounding against it like a wrecking ball.

"He's burning hot," Aunt Selma whispered. "This is bad."

Uncle Mike dried the pan and hung it on a hook on the wall.

"He's got it, hon," he said. "What's to be done? He's got it."

"We've got to get him to a hospital, Mike."

"What, so he can be around other sick folk?" Uncle Mike said. "Surrounded by the dead and the dying? The hospitals are no good to anyone right now. They don't even have enough doctors and nurses to keep up with the poor tramps that are winding up there."

Selma's face fell. "But— "

"No, no," Uncle Mike continued, "that little boy is safest in that bed, in that room. I just pray Barry brings his sister home soon before she catches something out there."

Aunt Selma began to cry. "What is happening?" she said, making a frustrated fist with her hand. "He's just a boy! And so young and healthy. At least . . . he *was*."

"Your sister was healthy, too, hon," Uncle Mike said. "I'm sure the Milanis were, too, until they brought that thing home with them."

"But why did they all get it, but not us? And not Barry?"

Uncle Mike shook his head. "Doesn't seem to be any rhyme or reason to this thing. But let's not speak too soon, either. We don't have anything *yet*."

Aunt Selma wiped the tears from her face. "Yes, of course—we're fine so far, by the grace of God and all that," she said.

Harry's coughing erupted again until it sounded like he was gagging. Aunt Selma looked at Mike. He turned around, grabbed the clean pan off the wall, and handed it to her.

"By the grace of God," she said again, then turned and went back into the bedroom.

Uncle Mike rapped his knuckles on the table.

"Knock on wood," he mumbled. "Just in case God's busy."

---

"I'm sorry, Barium," Harriet said, turning away from him and gazing back over at the wagon that held her parents. "I have to see them. You should have let me see them."

"Harriet, I'm sorry, but . . . I don't think you should."

**At Holy Cross Cemetery in Philadelphia, adult- and child-sized coffins were piled up in a horse shed, in anticipation of the delivery of more bodies.**

"Why? They're my parents! I want to . . ." Tears flowed down her cheeks. She shook her head and wept.

She had run all the way there, trailing the wagon that took her parents away from their apartment on South Street like so much luggage. She'd fallen a few times on the pavement and skinned her knee, but she hadn't even felt the pain. She'd just gotten back up and kept running, ignoring Barium as he called to her from behind. She'd felt like she could run forever, like she would never get tired, like her legs would never wear out. Now she was here, at the cemetery, and she wasn't ready to be. She wanted to run much farther. She wanted to run until she herself collapsed and died.

Barium hugged Harriet as she cried. She finally looked up, warily eyeing the wagonload of bodies less than ten feet in front of her. It was the wagon she'd followed here. That's where they were.

Barium gazed over at the crowd and, beyond them, to the young men who seemed to be digging a trench, like in newspaper photos of the soldiers fighting in Europe. He locked eyes with one who was standing by the mass grave, his shovel leaning on his shoulder. Barium gestured for the young man to come assist him.

Tim stepped forward hesitantly, unsure what the boy wanted from him, unsure if he wanted to get involved at all. The boy cocked his head toward the young girl, guiding Tim's eyes to her. Seeing her approaching the wagon of corpses, Tim suddenly realized what the boy was trying to do—or rather, what he was trying to stop the girl from doing. She was trying to look in the back of the wagon. But whomever she might be looking for, that person was now gone, nothing but a bloated corpse in its place. A girl her age shouldn't—couldn't—see such a thing. No one should.

Tim sprinted to the wagon, where some of his fellow volunteers, including Thomas, were starting to unload the bodies.

Barium watched as a body he recognized was unloaded from the pile: Harriet's friend Susanna. He gripped Harriet tighter to make sure she couldn't turn and look.

"Hello," Tim said, approaching Harriet and Barium, who now stood a few feet away from the wagon. "We're working here, I'm afraid. Something I can help you with?"

"My parents . . . ," Harriet began, but she couldn't get the words out.

"She wants to see her parents . . . before they're buried," Barium said, but he shook his head pointedly: *No, no, no.*

"Oh, I see." Tim nodded. He put his hand on Harriet's shoulder and guided her a few steps away, careful to keep her back to the wagon. "Sweetheart, I'm afraid that's not possible. It's an emergency situation, and we've got to get all of these poor souls buried before pestilence takes hold. It's not safe for you to be around the bodies."

"But that's them right there," Harriet said, sobbing anew and pointing out the figures of her parents in the back of the wagon. The bodies had shifted during the trip, and their legs were now visible beneath the sheets they were wrapped in. The familiar tufts of her mother's brown hair and the blue ribbon were blowing in the breeze on the opposite end.

"Harriet, no," Barium said, turning her around and placing his hands on her shoulders. "You don't want to see them."

"Why?" She couldn't believe Barium was saying what he was saying.

Barium sighed.

"I'm just going to tell you the truth," Barium began, biting his lip lest it begin to shake. "I saw my mom, Harriet. I came home and saw her after she was already gone. It was awful. I can't get the picture out of my head. She looked like a monster."

Barium averted his head to wipe the tears from his face.

"Please, Harriet. Please. You don't want to see them. You want to remember them as they were."

Having overheard the conversation, Thomas sidled over to Tim and whispered in his ear. Tim nodded, and as Barium and Harriet talked, Thomas crept over to the wagon and climbed up on the back wheel. He reached in and, after a few seconds of feeling around, pulled something from under one of the sheets. He then jumped down and passed the object to Tim, who walked over to Harriet and held it out to her.

"I'm so sorry," Tim said. "God bless you and keep you."

Harriet looked down at Tim's hand. He held her mother's blue ribbon. A piece of what was now the past. A piece of her mother that she could take with her.

Harriet's eyes filled with tears again, and she bowed her head, nodding her thanks.

"Good-bye," she whispered.

---

In Leo's room at the St. Charles infirmary, Sister Margaret, slumped in a chair next to his bed, opened her eyes. She looked in her lap, where her hands were cradling a Bible that she'd been reading to him.

She remembered reading the verses aloud as Leo lay immobile, his eyes glazed, his entire body covered in a dank wetness, his nostrils crusted over with dried blood, his chest slowly rising and falling as he struggled to breathe. She must have fallen asleep. She rubbed her eyes and looked out the window. The sun was out and a light breeze animated the trees. Suddenly the phone in the office rang. Standing up to go answer it, she looked down at Leo. She lowered her mask and let it hang from her neck.

His face was so dark he looked as if he'd escaped from a fire. His mouth and eyes were wide open. But his chest was no longer rising and falling.

The phone kept ringing—it somehow seemed to be getting louder.

Sister Margaret knelt down beside Leo, put her mask back over her mouth once again, and bowed to give him a kiss on the forehead.

As she prayed, the phone stopped ringing.

———————

At the Holy Cross Cemetery office, Tim hung up the telephone receiver. He walked outside and watched as Harriet departed the cemetery, holding her mother's ribbon, Barium at her side. He went to the wagon to meet Thomas, who was arriving back to fetch another body.

"Did you get through?" Thomas asked.

Tim shook his head.

"No answer."

# 8

# VERMIN

"THAT WAS QUITE A BLOW you took." Rachel wrapped Sister Katherine's head with a gauze bandage in the makeshift nurses' station. "Bonnie sure went down with a fire in her belly."

Sister Katherine cracked a furtive smile at Rachel's macabre joke. Bonnie had indeed gone down—dying just minutes later, squirming and spitting until her last breath. The glass pitcher she had hit Sister Katherine with had broken apart at the handle when it hit her head, and Bonnie had slashed the nun's cheek with the remaining shard.

"Yes, she was frightfully strong for such a sick woman," Sister Katherine said. "Thankfully she didn't have such great aim."

"Well, it was good enough, I suppose." Rachel snipped the gauze with the medical scissors and folded it under Sister Katherine's chin. "It's just good that your nursing cap was there to blunt the blow a little bit. Okay, I think the blood is beginning to clot. How's your head?"

Sister Katherine tilted her head slightly. "It's not too bad." In truth she'd never had such a terrible headache—she could feel her blood pumping inside her skull. But she was alive. More importantly, given where she'd been spending her days for the past week, she still wasn't sick. "If you could get me a drink of water, I'd be very grateful. Then I'll get back to my rounds. I'm sure Dr. Lawrence could use some help back up in the acute ward."

"If he hasn't slipped out the back door, that is," Rachel said with concern as she filled a cup from the sink and handed it to the nun. "Poor thing. He's barely out of school. Talk about 'out of the frying pan and into the fire.' He came all the way from Chestnut Hill to help."

"He's heeded God's call," Sister Katherine said, pressing the wrapped-up wound on her cheek gently. "Bless him."

"Well, he heeded someone's call, that's for sure," Rachel said. "Probably Wilmer Krusen's. Now, Sister, are you ready? We're short nurses again today, and we don't want a riot breaking out around poor Dr. Lawrence."

Sister Katherine stood and looked at her reflection in a small mirror behind the sink. The bandage went all across her cheek, down under her chin, up and over the top of her head, and back down to her cheek again.

"I suppose I'll blend in a little better now, with the bandage and all," she said as Rachel slid open the curtain and they stepped out into the hallway.

"Not until you start turning blue, Sister," Rachel joked darkly.

———✦———

Thomas's sleeping head lolled onto Tim's shoulder, jolting him out of his reverie. They were on a bus that was taking them from the Elwyn train station to a local school where they would be helping to care for children stricken with influenza. Tim quietly assured himself that he had made the right decision to go to Monsignor Drumgoole and ask that he and Thomas be reassigned.

"This job seems to be taking a toll on Thomas, sir," Tim had told the monsignor.

"As is the case for most of the volunteers, I imagine," Monsignor Drumgoole had said with apparent irritation. "But I tell you what: the Pennsylvania Training School for Feeble-Minded Children has a request in for volunteers to help them deal with their increasing number of cases. Apparently in the past week the school staff has found themselves crushed under the burden. I'm sending a small group out today—may as well give you a few days off from *this* grim work."

So Tim and Thomas handed over their shovels and boarded the train to Elwyn with four other seminarians. Their hearts were lightened by the prospect of spending a few days among children, however sick they were.

"Apparently they've got about twelve hundred children total, and more than eight hundred of them are sick," said one of the other student volunteers on the bus.

"Yeah." Another student nodded. "But it's little kids, right? It'll be a cakewalk compared to what we've *been* doing."

Tim thought so, too. And when he'd told Thomas the good news, he could almost see a burden being lifted off his friend's shoulders. Sure, they'd have to be careful about wearing their masks and making sure their hands were always clean. And, as Monsignor Drumgoole said, they were to do everything they were told by the nurses. But at least they wouldn't be having to slide slimy, decomposing body after slimy, decomposing body into the ground, over and over and over again until they were sick from the stench and half-crazy from the hopelessness of it all.

Thomas shook in his sleep, knocking his head against the window. He opened his eyes wearily and looked over at Tim.

"Another bad dream?" Tim asked.

"Nah, not too bad," Thomas said softly. "Just dreamed I was chasing my dog. And he didn't even have the flu." He looked at Tim and smiled weakly.

Tim slapped Thomas on the knee. "That's the spirit!"

The bus pulled into the school's circular driveway. It was a pristine stone building surrounded by lush greenery. A cobbled path led from the parking area to the main entrance. A small group of nurses emerged from the front door, followed by a tall man in dark brown slacks and black shirtsleeves. He gently pushed through the crowd of nurses and strode up to the vehicle. The six volunteers exited the bus, and the man extended a hand to Tim.

"You must be from St. Charles," he said. "I'm Father Lawrence Deerling. I'm pastor of the Church of the Nativity down the road. Been helping out however I can here."

Tim shook Father Deerling's hand. "Nice to meet you, Father. I'm Tim. We're ready to be put to work however you need us."

Father Deerling led the young men into the school and introduced them to the small staff of nurses.

"They've had a lot of nurses and attendants leave for better positions elsewhere. Less repellent ones, I suppose."

Tim wondered how medical professionals could even consider leaving sick children behind, no matter how awful the circumstances.

"They turned some of the larger rooms into wards—the gymnasium is the largest," Father Deerling said. He looked gravely at the seminarians. "The spread of this thing has been pretty ferocious. And lightning fast."

"How many deaths?" Thomas asked.

Father Deerling bristled slightly at the question. "None yet, thank the Lord. God has been merciful."

"How many doctors do you have?" Tim asked.

Father Deerling looked at Tim grimly. "I'm afraid just one. So you can see why we need your help."

Tim nodded. "We all do regular work with children at the seminary, so hopefully we can provide them some comfort." He smiled, and Father Deerling gave him a curious expression that made him wonder if he'd misspoken.

Father Deerling led Tim, Thomas, and the other volunteers into the gymnasium. It was filled to capacity with beds, and the cavernous room echoed with the querulous moaning and sandpaper coughing of one hundred patients. A few of them heard the doors swing open and turned their heads. The seminarians stopped in their tracks.

Gazing over at the person on the bed closest to him, Thomas went pale. A small person stared back expectantly, his dark eyes deeply set beneath a giant forehead that covered half of his malformed face. Splotches of dark hair sprouted wildly all over the lower half of his face, and his eyes were sunken deeply into the skin above his swollen cheeks.

"Welcome!" he yelped excitedly. He clapped his fingerless hands and smiled widely with his gaping, toothless mouth.

---

Wilmer wearily approached the entrance of Emergency Hospital No. 8 and pushed the doors open. He told himself this would be the last of his rounds for the day. He'd been to the Navy Yard, Blockley Hospital, Municipal Hospital, Broad Street, and Holmesburg. He had to get home, if only to calm his wife's nerves about the state of his own health, given the amount of exposure he'd had to the dead and dying.

"You can only do so much, Will," she'd said to him sternly before he left early that morning. It was true, he thought. His powers were painfully slight in the face of this epidemic. But what he could do—what he felt he *had* to do—was to witness this plague from the inside, to record it, to try somehow to learn from it. He was a scientist, after all.

Inside the hospital, he pushed open the door to the acute ward and gasped from the stench. He grabbed his mask and pressed it against his nose and mouth. Guttural moans and hacking coughs ricocheted off the walls and echoed through the large room. The young Dr. Lawrence was walking among the beds with his clipboard, mask over his mouth, bending and mumbling words to the patients to check responsiveness. In the far corner Wilmer saw Sister Katherine and Rachel administering to a couple of women lying in neighboring cots.

"Good evening, Dr. Krusen," Rachel said before returning to her task. Wilmer watched as Sister Katherine and Rachel brushed the women's hair. Clumps of it came out in the brushes and fell onto the floor, gathering in stringy clumps under the cots. Suddenly one of the women began to cough and shake uncontrollably. Sister Katherine calmly set the hairbrush down and lifted the woman's head up slightly to keep her from choking while she coughed.

The woman's coughing became stronger and began to thrust her forward. Sister Katherine could tell from the gargling sound in the woman's throat that she would be spitting something grotesque out of her mouth. The ferocious coughing soon turned into the sounds of suffocation. The woman flailed around as she gasped for breath. Sister Katherine held her by the shoulders as Rachel took her by the head and squeezed the woman's cheeks with the fingers and thumb of one hand to force her mouth to stay open. Then she reached a finger in to clear the passageway.

"I feel something," Rachel said, breathless. "Hold her, Sister."

Rachel forced two fingers in, then her thumb. "I've got it."

"It?" Sister Katherine said.

"Just keep holding." Wilmer scuttled over to help keep the woman down.

On the other side of the ward, Dr. Lawrence heard the commotion and looked up from his clipboard. He sighed and wiped sweat from his forehead before moving on to the next patient in the row of beds.

Rachel slowly withdrew her finger from the woman's mouth. Wrapped around the tip of her index finger was a worm. She kept pulling, and the slimy vermin continued to emerge.

"Oh, dear Lord," Sister Katherine whispered.

Rachel began to tug with both hands, one over the other, until the entire worm had been extracted. It was three feet long. Rachel gagged behind her mask, then leaped up and bolted to the nurses' station with the worm in her hands.

Sister Katherine and Wilmer let go of the woman, who collapsed back onto her cot, breathing more easily, though no less noisily.

"Excuse me, Doctor," Sister Katherine said, rising from the chair. "I'm going to go see if Nurse Rachel needs any . . . help with that."

**Sewage and trash in an alley behind houses on Hancock Street in Philadelphia, where severe sanitation problems contributed to the intensity of the influenza epidemic**

"Sister!" Wilmer cried. "Has that . . . happened before? Worms?"

"I don't believe so," Sister Katherine replied, shaking her head.

"I understand the situation is dire," he said. "But I must insist you make sure the premises are kept clean."

"We keep *the premises* plenty clean, Doctor." Returning to the woman's bed with a wet cloth, Rachel had to fight the urge to roll her eyes. "But we also don't turn patients away for showing up dirty. We treat everyone we have space for. That means, unfortunately, that we're caring for some folks who've been living in the streets"—she glared at Wilmer—"*where the worms live.*"

"I'm sorry," Wilmer stammered. "I do understand. I just . . . has there been another incident involving vermin?"

"Not that I've seen," Rachel said. She bent to wipe the woman's mouth and face. "But I wouldn't be surprised if it happens again. This part of town is filthy, as you know."

"I assure you we're doing everything we can to keep the ward hygienic, Doctor," Sister Katherine said.

"Of course, I know you are," Wilmer said. He looked over at Dr. Lawrence, who was now standing next to a cot five rows away. "How's young Dr. Lawrence doing?"

"He's been wonderful," Sister Katherine said. "But the poor thing hasn't stopped working since he got here. Not even taken a break. I think he's on his fifty-sixth hour now."

Wilmer furrowed his brow. "Well, I'm here now, and I'll stay as long as you need me. Maybe I can convince him to go into the office and get some shut-eye."

As if in response to Wilmer's proposal, Dr. Lawrence looked up from his clipboard, swayed back and forth a few times on wobbly legs, and fell face-first onto the floor.

———

Harriet and Barium walked slowly down South Street toward Aunt Selma and Uncle Mike's apartment. All the doors on the street had at least one piece of crepe tied to the knob to mark the death of someone inside—black for adults, gray for the elderly, and white for children. The two children passed a few neighborhood men loading bodies into wagons and other men in city uniforms collecting trash and spraying the sidewalks with water hoses.

They came to the door of the apartment building. Harriet noted that there was no crepe on the knob as she pushed the door open—that meant there had still been no deaths in the building. They crept down the dark hallway and up the stairs to the apartment. Inside, the main room was dark, and Aunt Selma and Uncle Mike were seated at the table in the kitchenette. Aunt Selma wiped tears from her eyes and leaped up, rushing over to the pair and hugging them both tightly.

"Oh, we were so worried!" she sobbed. She placed her hands on the sides of Harriet's head and tilted the girl's head up. "Darling, are you all right?"

Harriet nodded.

"Did you . . . see them?"

"No," Barium answered quickly. "But she . . . said good-bye."

"And," Harriet added, "one of the cemetery men gave me this." She held out her mother's blue ribbon.

Aunt Selma stroked Harriet's hair and wiped a tear from the girl's face.

"That's beautiful," she said.

"We should find a safe place for you to keep it," Uncle Mike said, standing up and ambling over. "I think I've got an old coin box you can use."

"Thank you," Harriet whispered. She looked over at the bedroom door. "Is Harry sleeping?"

"Yes," Aunt Selma answered. "Been sleeping ever since you left. Except for once when I woke him to give him some turpentine with sugar. I don't know if it'll help, but my mother always swore by it. He coughed a bit"—Aunt Selma's eyes darted quickly over to Uncle Mike, then back—"but he went back to sleep soon after."

Harriet exhaled a sigh of relief.

"Has he eaten anything?" Barium asked.

Aunt Selma shook her head. "Only the turpentine and sugar. But we'll try to give him some soup a little later."

"Can I go in and see him?" Harriet asked.

Aunt Selma and Uncle Mike looked at each other.

"Sure, honey. But best not to get too close to him. We don't want to disturb his sleep and . . . you don't want to catch anything. Here, put this on." Aunt Selma walked across the room and pulled a new medical mask out of a drawer by the couch.

Barium helped Harriet tie the mask around her face, and Uncle Mike approached the bedroom door. He peeked in, then turned to Aunt Selma and nodded.

Her medical mask snug if slightly lopsided, Harriet slowly stepped into the room. It was dark, with only a tiny window next to the bed allowing light inside. She could hear Harry's raspy breathing, and as she stepped closer to the bed she felt heat radiating from his body and smelled the pungent scent of turpentine. She fingered her mother's ribbon, which was still in her hand, and remembered that her brother still didn't know the truth about their parents.

She knelt by the bed. "Hi, Harry," she whispered. "It's your sister."

Harry's labored breathing continued. He wheezed in and out, in and out, in and out.

"I'm sorry I went away this morning. I had to . . . go see Mommy and Daddy. Mommy gave me something—I'll show it to you later, when you're better." A few tears rolled down her

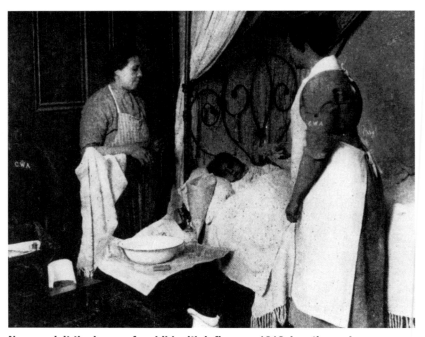

**Nurses visit the home of a child with influenza, 1918, location unknown.**

cheeks and dampened the mask covering her mouth. "I'll stay here from now on, until you're well, okay? Gonna take care of you, I promise."

She could see the silhouette of her brother's face, and the rising and falling of his chest. His hair looked wet, like it was plastered to his forehead.

"And Barium can't wait 'til you're well enough to go outside again and toss the ball around. He's been a really great friend."

She wanted so badly to hear her brother say something— even something rude or inappropriate, like usual—but she knew that there was no way to make that happen. As if giving confirmation that she would just have to wait, Harry suddenly coughed, lifting his head off the pillow and holding it for a few seconds, then letting it fall back down. *Maybe he'll be better tomorrow,* she thought.

Harriet got to her feet and prepared to leave, then spontaneously bent to turn on the bedside table lamp.

The lamp was small and only offered a dim light, but it was enough for Harriet to see her brother's sleeping face. She tilted her head as she looked at him. He looked different. His face had darkened since she'd last seen him.

It almost looked a little blue.

# An Uncanny Population

THOMAS FROZE as the excited "child" who had just addressed him continued to bounce on his mattress and clap.

All six St. Charles volunteers looked around at the patients, who, having noted the arrival of new helpers from the outside world, were slowly coming to life and moving around in their beds. Enormous misshapen heads emerged from underneath bedsheets, as did tiny heads shaped like sacks of potatoes and round heads with oversize ears. Some were grown men with beards and long legs. Others were mere boys with oversize, deformed heads. Most shockingly, there were many others who, though scarcely the size of five-year-old boys, had patches of facial hair and weathered, craggy faces, and they grumbled and guffawed in low-pitched, gravelly voices.

Tim and Thomas had accepted their new assignment with relief, eager to get away from the stench of death and the endless, grisly parade of decomposing bodies. This job, they had thought, would allow them the chance to work with the living—children with beating hearts and playful spirits. But the gymnasium was a frightful hall of mirrors that mocked their expectations.

Tim gazed over at Thomas and saw his look of utter shock. He feared that Thomas was ready to panic and bolt out the door—or even the window—to escape the freakish group of patients gazing at them. He rushed over to Thomas and took him gently by the arm.

"Thomas," he whispered, "take a breath."

Thomas sucked in a mouthful of air with a hiss and exhaled slowly.

"Let's go say hello to him." Tim gestured to the patient who had greeted them so enthusiastically. Thomas attempted to wriggle his arm free of Tim's grip, but Tim tightened his grasp, looked Thomas in the eyes, and slowly shook his head.

"Calmly, Thomas, calmly. Look at him—he's harmless."

The man continued to move around excitedly on the bed, ably rearranging himself into a sitting position with his fingerless hands and folding his short legs underneath him. He smiled and smacked his lips as he wiped saliva from his mouth.

"And it looks like he's eager to meet us."

Tim and Thomas approached the bed, and as they did, the man swayed quickly back and forth in anticipation.

"Hi there. I'm Tim and this is Thomas. What's your name?"

"I'm Georgie," he said. His speech was cloudy, as if his tongue were made of cotton. He tapped his chest with his hand. "Georgie."

Tim couldn't tell how old Georgie was—his grizzled face suggested middle age, though he was certainly a child mentally.

"How are you feeling, Georgie?" Tim asked.

"Mmmm," Georgie mumbled, tilting his head. "It hot. And I need to pee."

Tim and Thomas couldn't help but snicker in spite of themselves. Georgie saw their reaction and began to sway back and forth more intensely.

"I need to pee!" He laughed. "I need to pee! NEEEEED PEEEEEE!" He suddenly sneezed, landing a gob of dark red phlegm at Tim's feet.

"Okay, Georgie, okay . . ." A nurse scurried over to the bed. "Sorry, he gets a little excitable," she said to Tim and Thomas.

"Maybe I should take him along to the washroom?" Tim said.

"Sure," the nurse replied. "He looks like he's taken a shine to you. Georgie, this nice man is going to go with you to the bathroom, okay? Now you be a good boy and don't do anything naughty in there."

"Okay! Okay!" Georgie hurled himself off the bed, elegantly landing on both feet. He was about three and a half feet tall, coming up only to Tim's stomach. "I need to pee!" he yelped, tapping Tim on the hip and bounding toward the door. Tim smiled nervously, nodded at Thomas, and hurried after his new charge.

"I'm sorry, young man," the nurse said, turning to Thomas. "I'm afraid perhaps you all had a different impression of what our facility is."

Looking around the room at the other four volunteers fanning out among the patients, Thomas nodded. "Ah, yes, I think we did have something else in mind when we heard our help was needed at a children's school," he said.

"Well, we do really appreciate your coming—this illness has certainly taken us over." The nurse led Thomas down along a row of beds. "It is quite an uncanny population here, as you can see. Most are adult men, though they're children in intelligence, with a few exceptions, like Isaac over there." She nodded at a man in a bed just a few rows over from Georgie's. He had a small, wrinkled head with large eyes that seemed ready to pop out of their sockets, and he was covered by a hospital gown that was far too big for him. Because the gown hid the man's legs so completely, Thomas couldn't tell if he was just sitting up in bed or if he was standing.

"Most of them are pretty good-natured, though being sick always throws them for a loop. Anyway, you'll want to wear one of these." She handed Thomas a medical mask and walked away.

Thomas strung the mask around his neck and let it hang there. He looked around and saw that Isaac was glaring at him.

"Hi there. My name's Thomas. It's nice to meet you."

"Should put it on," Isaac said, his voice the timbre of a little boy's. Thomas looked down and realized Isaac was referring to the mask hanging from his neck.

"Oh, this?" Thomas said.

"Yeah." Isaac smirked. "Oughta put it on."

Thomas smiled nervously as he placed the mask over his nose and mouth and tightened the strings.

"How's this?" he asked, his words slightly muffled.

Isaac nodded. "Definitely improves your appearance."

* * *

Barium stood in the doorway of the apartment building, looking out at an older lady who lived next door. She was sitting on her stoop with her head in her hands, sobbing. Behind her, a piece of white crepe fluttered on the doorknob. Barium backed into the hallway and returned to his aunt and uncle's apartment.

Inside, all was quiet, though the silence was punctured periodically by the sounds of coughing and sneezing. Barium poked his head into the bedroom; nothing had changed. Aunt Selma lay on the far side of the bed, Harry was in the middle, and Harriet was curled up at the near edge, sleeping with her head resting against her brother's stomach. Uncle Mike lay on a pile of newspapers spread out on the hard wooden floor, sleeping on his back.

They were all sick now.

Harriet had started showing symptoms soon after she and Barium had returned from the cemetery. She'd stayed with Harry all night, kneeling at the side of the bed, applying Vicks to his chest and under his nose, and wiping the perspiration from his face with a cloth from the kitchen. She remained there even as she herself began coughing and running a fever. Soon enough, Aunt Selma and Uncle Mike were both unable to even sit upright and had taken to the bedroom in almost a hypnotized state, not responding to any of Barium's questions.

And yet Barium wasn't sick at all. He'd never felt a single symptom. He felt the same today as he did on the day of the Liberty Loan Parade, the same as he'd felt the day before that and the day before that. How had he escaped this sickness, without even trying? He'd been surrounded by it now for almost two weeks. His mother, his neighbors—death encircled him. Yet there he stood, healthy as a horse, as the life drained out of everyone around him.

Barium went back outside to take a walk. He headed down South Street toward Broad Street. It was completely deserted—a few wagons collecting bodies had just departed for the cemetery. Every doorknob he passed had crepe hanging from it, most of it white. So many young people dying. Barium stopped in front of his school friend Chris Tung's building. The Tung family's tenement was on the first floor, and Barium hadn't seen any member of the family in well over a week. They weren't very social around the neighborhood—the parents didn't speak any English, only Chinese, so their children had to translate even the shortest of conversations.

Barium couldn't stop himself from peeking in the Tungs' window. All was dark, and nobody stirred inside. He stepped over and pushed open the front door, which was barely clinging to its hinges. Moving quietly down the hallway toward the Tungs' apartment, Barium told himself he'd just make sure everything was okay. He stepped to the door and saw that it was open a crack. Poking his head in, he saw an empty sitting room. The layout of the apartment was similar to his aunt and uncle's—one sitting room, a tiny kitchenette, and a bedroom. He stepped in.

"Hello? Anyone here?" He suddenly heard the sound of footsteps in the bedroom. He strode over to the bedroom door and knocked.

"Hello?" There was no sound. He knocked again and then, after a few seconds, turned the doorknob and pushed.

The reek of decomposition engulfed him as he opened the door, and he tumbled backward onto the floor. On his hands and knees, he gagged and heaved, trying to suppress the urge to vomit as his stomach churned. Then he heard the sound of something slam against one of the bedroom walls. He turned to look, but the room was dark. Lifting his shirt and pressing it against his nose and mouth, Barium once again stepped into the bedroom. Nervously he felt for the light switch on the wall and flicked it.

Mr. and Mrs. Tung lay on the bed, their faces covered in blood. Chris lay beside them, holding his younger sister in his arms. Both were bloated and blue. How long had they been dead? Barium heard a gasp and turned his head toward the door to the little closet on the far wall. He walked calmly forward, still holding his shirt against his nose and mouth. He opened the door, and his shirt fell from his face.

Five-year-old Jesse was huddled in the back of the closet, wide-eyed and shivering.

———•◦•———

Sister Katherine moved among the cots, offering towels, water, and, every few minutes, prayers for the dying. She stopped over the body of a young man who'd appeared to be just back from the war when he'd arrived yesterday. He was now gone—having survived the Germans, he lasted less than twenty-four hours in the ward. Sister Katherine bowed her head, closed her eyes, and whispered a quick benediction. A pair of orderlies hurried over to remove the body while Sister Katherine stripped the bed.

It seemed that every day there was an entirely new roster of patients at the hospital taking over the unhappy beds of the previous occupants, who were now lying in a heap outside the building. The deadhouse was filled to capacity, so the bodies were now piling up on the hospital grounds. Immediately upon arriving, Wilmer had assembled a dedicated staff of orderlies whose only job would be to keep the dead moving out and the still-alive moving in.

Like clockwork, Rachel arrived with new bedsheets just as Sister Katherine had finished pulling the discolored and putrid-smelling ones off. They then traded jobs, Rachel taking over the bed duties as Sister Katherine scurried away to toss the old sheets into a large laundry chute. She paused for a moment, took a breath, and turned back around. She saw Dr. Lawrence in the first row of beds, lying on his back. He was as wet as a fish and shivering, mumbling words that she couldn't understand.

Her heart sank as she looked at him. His face was damp and dark, and his lips were cracked. He'd been perfectly healthy yesterday—a strapping young doctor, daunted by the fearsome disease he had to treat, but eager to help and hungry for the experience. She had witnessed for herself his lightning-fast deterioration—one moment he had been standing among the cots jotting notes on his clipboard, the next he was unconscious on the floor with blood spewing from his nostrils. Now here he was, talking to himself like a ninety-year-old man.

"Grim day," Rachel said, padding up to the nurses' station.

"I just can't believe how fast he's going," Sister Katherine said. "He was so fit. Reminded me of some of the students at St. Charles."

Rachel washed her hands and splashed water on her face.

"Sister," she said as she patted her face dry with a towel, "I guess you know God pretty well, don't you?"

Sister Katherine's face turned quizzical. "Well, I try to. I talk to him every day."

"Well, next time you talk to him, can you ask him something for me? Just ask him this: Why? Why is he letting this happen?"

Sister Katherine was quiet, unsure of what to say.

"Do you think he'll answer you? Do you think he *has* an answer?"

Sister Katherine looked away and gazed over at the bodies of the sick. She slowly shook her head. "I . . . I just don't know. There's much we can't know, that we have to leave up to God's—"

"Plan, I know," Rachel interrupted. She shook her head at Sister Katherine. "I've heard that a lot from all the nuns I've talked to. We're just supposed to say our useless prayers and hope that he's paying attention. But ask yourself: How could God's plan involve this?" Rachel gestured at the sea of patients. "Is this part of the plan? All those poor mommas and babies in the deadhouse?"

Sister Katherine bowed her head slightly, unable to look at Rachel, whose voice was now trembling. Rachel wiped tears from her eyes and placed a hand on Sister Katherine's shoulder.

"I'm sorry, Sister. I know you can't possibly have all the answers. I just wonder if it makes you wonder."

Sister Katherine raised her head again and looked into Rachel's eyes. "It does, Nurse Rachel. And I do." A tear ran down her cheek. "All I can do is hold tightly to my faith that there is a plan. And that we just don't know it."

The two women hugged. It was the first physical contact they'd had in their many days of working together. Afterward, Rachel went back to her rounds, walking among the cots, grimly checking the status of the sick. Sister Katherine went to see if Dr. Lawrence needed anything.

Leaning over his bed, she stopped cold. She looked around for an orderly, but there were none nearby. So she pulled the sheet over his face, bowed her head, and began what Rachel would call another useless prayer.

———•—•——

Barium knelt down and reached his hand to Jesse, who was crouched in the back corner of the closet. He couldn't tell if the boy was shivering because he was cold, sick, or terrified. Maybe all three.

"Hi, Jesse. It's me, Barium. Here, take my hand."

Jesse shook his head frantically. Barium took a deep breath through his mouth, struggling to keep from retching at the stench of the corpses around him. He moved a little closer to the closet.

"Jesse," he said softly, "you're going to be okay. I'll take you somewhere safe."

Barium reached in, but Jesse squirmed out of reach, pressing himself against the back of the closet and upsetting a stack of small shoeboxes, which came tumbling down. A pair of boys' black shoes rolled out of one of them.

*Chris's shoes,* Barium thought. He looked back at the bed, where Chris lay with his sister in his arms. He immediately tried to push the image of his friend from his mind.

"Jesse," he said, reaching in again. "Don't you want to go outside? Aren't you hungry? I can get you some food."

Jesse swallowed slowly and gazed at Barium with pleading eyes. Barium saw his chance to coax the boy out.

"My aunt Selma's made soup, and we've got bread from the store." He could see Jesse's mouth watering at the mention of food. But still the boy didn't move.

"Yeah, soup, and . . . I think she's making cookies," Barium lied. Aunt Selma and Uncle Mike didn't even have an oven.

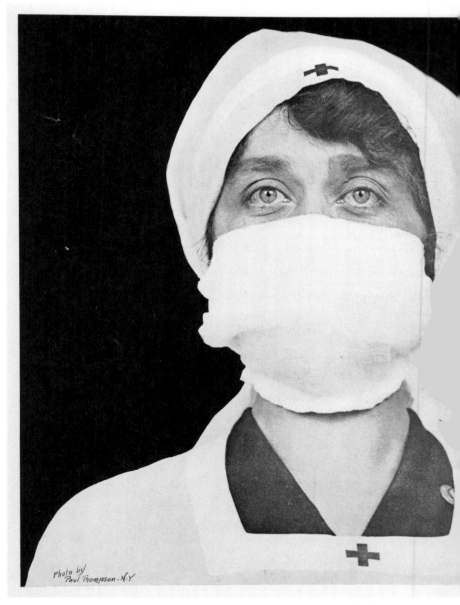

A 1918 notice on how to avoid the flu. Doctors did not understand influenza as well as they do today, but avoiding common drinking cups and covering one's mouth remain good advice.

# To Prevent
# Influenza!

Do not take any person's breath.

Keep the mouth and teeth clean.

Avoid those that cough and sneeze.

Don't visit poorly ventilated places.

Keep warm, get fresh air and sunshine.

Don't use common drinking cups, towels, etc.

Cover your mouth when you cough and sneeze.

Avoid Worry, Fear and Fatigue.

Stay at home if you have a cold.

Walk to your work or office.

In sick rooms wear a gauze mask like in illustration.

"Come on, Jesse, you can do it. Let's go get some dinner. I'll carry you."

Jesse crawled forward slowly, his eyes darting around as the room outside the closet started coming into view. Barium pulled Jesse close and pressed his head tightly against his chest, putting his hand over the boy's eyes so Jesse wouldn't see his family's bodies lying on the bed. He stood and carefully crept out of the room, closing the door behind him.

Harriet placed a dry cloth on Harry's forehead to soak up the sweat that had accumulated there like raindrops on an umbrella. Aunt Selma opened the door and stepped into the bedroom. She was hunched over, dressed in a robe, and coughing.

"How you feeling, honey?" she asked Harriet, placing her hand on the girl's forehead. "You're still hot."

Harriet wiped her nose. "I feel okay, just tired."

"I've made some more soup. Uncle Mike's out in the kitchen. Why don't you go get something to eat while Harry's sleeping?"

"Where's Barium?"

"Not sure. Maybe went for a walk."

Harriet looked down at her brother. His face was wet, swollen, and bruise colored.

"Okay," she said. "You'll sit with him?"

"'Course I will, honey."

Harriet stood and wrapped a small blanket around her shoulders. "I'll be back in a few minutes." She closed the door behind her.

When Harriet had finished her small bowl of soup, she fell asleep on the sofa in the main room. Uncle Mike covered her with another blanket and returned to the bedroom. Aunt Selma was still in the chair by the bed. She was stroking Harry's hair and whispering something to him.

As Uncle Mike collapsed onto the other side of the bed, Harry opened his eyes.

"Harry?" Aunt Selma said. "Harry, can you see me?"

"Harriet," he said weakly. His eyes moved back and forth, back and forth. He moved his head on the pillow, too: back and forth, back and forth. "Harriet."

He died with his sister's name on his lips.

# UNDER THE DOGWOOD TREE

"So, HOW LONG HAVE YOU been sick?" Thomas sat down next to Isaac and handed him a glass of water. Thomas and Tim had just visited every bed in the gymnasium, bringing the patients water, cold compresses, and prayers. Now they were both taking a break to visit with their favorite "children"—Tim sat at Georgie's bed a few rows over.

"Brought me in here yesterday," Isaac huffed. "Felt like a washed-up fish, flopping about with my mouth open, trying to breathe, sweating whole bodies of water."

"Can I ask you a question?"

"You've already asked me a question," Isaac replied, staring at Thomas curiously, his large eyes bulging. "Actually, you asking me if you can ask me . . . that makes two questions."

"Ha, okay," Thomas said. "Can I ask you *another* question?"

"Okay, one more."

"Why are you here? At this school? You seem—"

"You mean why aren't I at Harvard with all the other hand-some geniuses?" Isaac made himself laugh with this statement, which brought on a coughing attack. A glob of brown phlegm splashed on his bedsheets as he tried to steady himself. His coughing finally stopped, though he remained hunched over and wheezing, breathing slowly and deliberately to keep from setting off another fit of coughing.

"Well, yeah, I suppose," Thomas said. "You don't seem to have the same . . . troubles as the others." Thomas looked around him and saw Georgie rocking back and forth, his nose leaking blood as Tim read to him from the Bible. Georgie lapped up the blood with his tongue as it trickled down to his lips. Tim stopped reading, grabbed a wet cloth, and pressed it to Georgie's face.

"If you haven't noticed," Isaac wheezed, "I'm more circus freak than scholar." He threw the sheet off his body and pulled up his gown.

In truth, Thomas had not noticed. But now he gazed down and saw that Isaac had no legs. His feet appeared to have grown right out of his pelvis. Isaac wiggled his toes at Thomas, who tried unsuccessfully not to flinch. "I wish I *were* dumb as a brick, actually—make life easier."

Georgie unleashed a raggedy cough, spraying blood and spittle onto Tim and his Bible.

"It would be nice, wouldn't it?" Isaac sighed. "Just be blissful and ignorant like old Georgie over there." He lay back onto his pillow, shivering. "He'll probably outlive me, the dumb bastard." He erupted in another fit of wet coughing.

"Where's your family?" Thomas asked as he handed a tissue to Isaac.

"More questions!" Isaac said in mock exasperation. "You are a very curious seminarian."

"Sorry," Thomas said, blushing.

"No, I don't mind. Your questions are much more polite than the ones I'm used to." Isaac issued a craggy cough, spit something into his tissue, and wiped his mouth. "I have no family—I sprang spontaneously from the head of Zeus a hundred and fifty years ago." Isaac looked at Thomas and wiggled his toes. "Only half of me made it out, but it was the good half."

Thomas didn't know how to react to this odd answer, so he just stared at Isaac and hoped a real answer was forthcoming.

"All right." Isaac sighed. "You're no fun at all. Truth be told, I was born in Allentown. It was always my dream to run away to someplace exotic like London or Paris. But as you can see, I don't run very fast, so here I am in this paradise we call Elwyn."

"No family?" Thomas asked.

"None to speak of," Isaac said as he lay back onto his pillow. "Or rather, none I care to speak of. I suppose my *family* is here." He gazed over at Georgie. "I guess that would make Georgie my little brother." As if on cue, Georgie erupted with a bellowing cough.

"Mr. Buckley." A nurse approached Tim at Georgie's bed as he wiped his face and his Bible of Georgie's recent torrent. "Monsignor Drumgoole is on the phone for you." Tim shot Thomas a look, then quickly followed her into the office.

"Is there anything you need?" Thomas whispered to Isaac, who was now lying with his eyes closed, still controlling his wheezing breathing lest he trigger another coughing attack. "Or . . . do you want me to read to you?"

"You got a copy of *Great Expectations* with you?" Isaac mumbled without opening his eyes.

"No." Thomas smiled. "I'm afraid I don't."

"Well, don't bother with the Bible. I already know how it ends."

Thomas sat still and silent for a few minutes, watching Isaac's chest rise and fall. Soon enough, Isaac was asleep.

All of a sudden Thomas felt a tap on his shoulder. He turned around and there was Tim, looking distracted.

"So what did Monsignor Drumgoole want? Don't tell me he's calling us back to the cemetery already."

"Well, kind of," Tim said. "But just to say good-bye." Tim looked over at Georgie, who was coughing in his sleep.

"Say good-bye? To who?"

"To Leo."

<hr/>

Harriet stood by the bed, looking down at Harry. Her face was wet with tears, her lips quivering. Uncle Mike sat on the opposite side of the bed with his back to Harriet, his head bobbing to and fro as he coughed. Aunt Selma moved over to help him stand, then walked with him out to the kitchen and held on to him as he sat down. Returning to the bedroom, she placed a hand on Harriet's shoulder and gazed down at Harry's body. His face was dark blue.

"Honey, we should . . . prepare him," Aunt Selma whispered. Harriet wiped her nose and coughed. She tugged her shoulder loose from Aunt Selma and knelt by the bed. She stroked her brother's hair and could feel that he was already turning cold. She planted a kiss on her open palm and placed it on Harry's head, then stood up.

"Prepare him how?" she asked.

Aunt Selma walked around the bed and reached for the sheet, grabbing and tossing the corners toward the middle of the mattress. She circled back around to where Harry lay and tugged the sheet over him. Before allowing it to cover his face, she paused, bent down, and kissed his head, then pulled the sheet until he disappeared under it.

"Uncle Mike can take him outside to the wagon," Aunt Selma said, stepping to the door.

"No," Harriet said.

Aunt Selma turned around.

"I don't want Harry just flopped onto a wagon with a bunch of other people," Harriet said. "He'll be crushed." She marched out to the main room, swung open the door, and stepped into the hallway.

"Harriet! Harriet, where are you going?"

A few minutes later Harriet emerged from the street, tugging behind her a large, empty wooden crate. It was about three feet long, with the words *Sunkist Oranges* printed on the side. She stepped over to the couch and grabbed the small blanket Uncle Mike had covered her with, then carefully lined the crate with it, preparing a soft cushion over the hard wood.

"Uncle Mike, can you help me with Harry?" she asked.

Uncle Mike, coughing and bleary-eyed, nodded. "Of course, hon."

Harriet opened the bedroom door for him, and soon after, Uncle Mike stepped through the threshold with Harry in his arms. Slowly, Uncle Mike knelt down beside the crate and placed Harry's body inside it, still enclosed in the bedsheet Aunt Selma had covered him with. Uncle Mike had to bend the boy's legs so that he could fit completely.

Harriet dragged the crate out to the hallway and then, with Uncle Mike's help, set it on the pavement outside. She sat down next to it and, head in her hands, waited for the next wagon to pass.

A few minutes later Uncle Mike joined her out on the sidewalk. "Hi, Barium," he said suddenly.

Harriet looked up: Barium walked slowly toward them, cradling in his arms their five-year-old neighbor Jesse from down the road. Jesse's eyes were closed.

She looked at the crate that held her brother's body, then back at Jesse. New tears sprang from her eyes, and her head sank back into her hands.

Barium lowered his head to Jesse's ear and whispered his name.

"Jesse, wake up. We're here."

Jesse lifted his head and looked around him. Catching Harriet's surprised gaze, he stared at her expectantly, as if she had important information to give him. But she just smiled.

"Hi, Jesse," she said. Jesse rubbed his eyes and gazed sleepily back at her.

"Uncle Mike," Barium said, "can you take Jesse inside? He needs to eat. There's no telling when he had food last."

"Sure thing," Uncle Mike said, reaching his hands out.

Jesse looked at Barium, and the older boy nodded. "It's okay, Jesse," he said. "This is my uncle Mike. He'll get you some soup." He handed the boy over to his uncle.

They went inside, leaving Barium standing over Harriet, who remained sitting on the pavement next to the orange crate that held Harry.

Barium noticed the crate and the white of the sheet inside. He opened his mouth to speak but quickly realized he had no words for this. He sat down next to Harriet and put his arm around her.

Soon they heard the crackle and grind of wagon wheels approaching. She stood and waved her hand to capture the driver's attention, and the wagon soon slowed to a stop in the middle of the road. Harriet saw that the back of the wagon contained only a few bodies.

"Barium, can you help?"

The two of them dragged the orange crate out to the wagon, then, with the driver's help, lifted it up and placed it in the back. Harriet immediately heaved herself into the wagon and flopped down next to the crate, her legs hanging off the back.

"Little lady, you can't ride in this," the driver said, taking his cap off and wiping his face with it before slapping it against his dungarees. "It's going to be full of bodies in a few minutes."

"Can you take us to the cemetery now?" Harriet gazed at the driver and then over at Barium.

"The wagon's nearly empty," the driver said.

"I want to take my brother to the cemetery now, though."

Barium stepped up and hopped into the back next to Harriet.

"She'll be okay back here," he said. "I'll be with her."

"There's lots of bodies to pick up," the driver said. "Don't want to waste a trip."

Harriet slumped over the crate, resting her head on the top while her arms draped over the sides. Barium stared at the driver imploringly. The driver looked from Harriet to Barium and then at the orange crate. With a respectful nod of his head, he put his cap back on, returned to the carriage, and grabbed the reins.

The wagon crept down the street, winding a path back to Holy Cross Cemetery.

———•—•———

"Is that right?" Wilmer Krusen was on the phone, sitting in the cluttered office at Emergency Hospital No. 8, where he'd spent the night.

"Yes, sir," the voice said on the other end of the line. "Calls for help dropped off materially today."

"Well, that's certainly welcome news," Wilmer said. He smiled for what felt to him like the first time in years. "Thank you, Officer."

He hung up the phone and excitedly wrote the police officer's comments into his notebook. He was glad he had called. When totaling the numbers from yesterday at No. 8, he'd seen that the number of new cases had decreased slightly. So he had called the local police precinct to find out what they were seeing. It had been a dog of a day yesterday—more people had died in the wards than any day previous, and every day promised a further increase. Now he saw a shift: fewer sick people came in.

*Numbers don't lie,* Wilmer thought. *But what about the other hospitals?*

Wilmer picked the phone up again and dialed Emergency Hospital No. 1.

"Yes, hello, this is Dr. Krusen with the health department. Yes, just wanting to get a quick read of your latest influenza numbers." As he waited Wilmer couldn't help but feel a flush of

# INFLUENZA IN PHILADELPHIA
## NEW CASES AND DEATHS, OCTOBER 1918

### 1918

| DATE | NEW CASES | DEATHS |
|------|-----------|--------|
| 10/4/18 | 636 | 139 |
| 10/6/18 | 788 | 171 |
| 10/8/18 | 1,481 | 250 |
| 10/10/18 | 5,531 | 361 |
| 10/11/18 | 4,013 | 517 |
| 10/14/18 | 4,302 | 557 |
| 10/16/18 | 2,280 | 650 |
| 10/17/18 | 1,686 | 711 |
| 10/20/18 | 1,334 | 606 |

Source: Eileen A. Lynch, "The Flu of 1918," The Pennsylvania Gazette
November/December 1998, www.upenn.edu/gazette/1198/lynch.html.

hope. Every day for the past two weeks the numbers of sick and dead citywide had only gone up.

"That's new cases, yes?" he said, scribbling in his notebook. "From yesterday? Thank you." Wilmer hung up, looked up the next number, and dialed. The emergency hospital at Holmesburg offered similar news, with one additional point: there were fewer new patients, yes; but also, fewer people had died.

Something was happening. For the next hour Wilmer phoned hospitals and police stations, collecting numbers that, for the first time in weeks, weren't eclipsing the numbers from the day before. Every person he talked to at the hospitals said the same thing: the total number of patients coming in with the flu decreased yesterday for the first time since the arrival of this plague. And the number of emergency calls to police stations across the city appeared to be declining.

Could it be true? Was the epidemic finally losing steam?

<hr />

Tim and Thomas walked through the crowded gates of Holy Cross and were surprised by what they saw. Their fellow seminarians were still there, but they were no longer digging trenches. A large steam shovel was digging a giant common grave, while some of the student volunteers carried bodies, coffins, and crates over to another nearby trench. They carefully passed them down to others standing in the eight-foot-deep hole, where the corpses were placed side by side. A few young men were crouched down under a dogwood tree, surrounded by a group of nuns from St. Charles dressed in nurse's coats.

"Hello, Monsignor," Tim said. He and Thomas approached Monsignor Drumgoole, who was surrounded by forlorn family members of the dead. The monsignor turned around.

"Boys, I'm glad you've come," he said. "Leo's body just arrived. Some of the boys have already dug a grave for him. He's over there." The monsignor turned his gaze to a fresh mound of earth under the dogwood tree. "Haven't got much time, I'm afraid. I think all of you are here now, so we should get started. As you can see, there are many more services to conduct."

The seminarians slowly gathered at the dogwood tree, dropping their shovels in silence and moving, ghostlike, to the grave. Tim and Thomas greeted their friends with reticent nods, shook hands, hugged. They all looked down at their

The Holy Cross Cemetery, outside Philadelphia, circa 1920s

friend Leo's body draped in a sheet. Flowers were strewn all over him.

More students gathered while Monsignor Drumgoole tried to extricate himself from the throng of mourners crowding around. Another wagon arrived, and the monsignor took advantage of the attention it attracted to back away and hurry over to Leo's gravesite. As he approached, the young seminarians who were gathered there—now numbering more than fifty—were already chanting the Benedictus. Their voices rose in the air, the collected and mournful harmonies bringing a hush to the other noises filling the cemetery. All talking ceased.

Harriet and Barium hopped down from the back of the arriving wagon. Harriet couldn't stop herself from following the sound of the singing to its source, as if she were pulled by an invisible string.

"Harriet, where are you going?" Barium asked. He watched her move slowly toward the dogwood tree, past the countless bodies scattered all over the grass, waiting to be buried. She passed a bony teenage boy, still dressed in his pajamas, with deep purple blotches on his arms and neck, and a young woman in a pink dress with crusted blood on her face.

A tear escaped Harriet's eye. But it wasn't a tear of sadness—not at this moment. The singing was the most beautiful she'd ever heard. If she were listening in the dark, or with her eyes closed, she would swear she was hearing the voices of angels. But she wasn't, and she could see that this gorgeous noise was coming from the young men up ahead, wearing overalls and dungarees, covered in dirt, mud, and sweat, and surrounded by the pungent reek of death.

Harriet stopped in her tracks—an idea popped into her head. She turned and ran back to the wagon. A few moments later she and Barium carried the orange crate across to where the seminarians and nuns were singing. Harriet sat down next to the crate, running her hand along its edge.

The singing came to an end, and Monsignor Drumgoole said a prayer. Tim looked over and noticed Harriet and Barium sitting on the ground just outside the circle of Leo's mourners. Recognizing Harriet from her previous visit to Holy Cross, he went to her. He knelt down and placed his hand on the crate.

"Your family?" he whispered.

"Brother," Harriet mumbled, nodding her head.

Tim peered at the area around the dogwood tree. He thought he spied just enough space for a small grave near Leo's.

Turning back to Harriet, Tim said, "How about your friend and I go make him a nice place to rest?" Harriet's eyes widened and she nodded thankfully, while Barium rose to his feet in agreement. As Monsignor Drumgoole finished his prayer and the seminarians once more raised their voices in song, the two took up shovels to dig a grave for Harry Milani.

---

Uncle Mike sat with Jesse at the small table in the kitchenette, wiping the boy's face of dirt, sweat, and grime with a wet cloth. Aunt Selma placed a bowl of soup in front of Jesse, sitting down next to him. Uncle Mike held on to the side of the boy's head and scrubbed.

"I think that'll do for now, little man," Uncle Mike said after a few minutes. He stood and stepped to the sink to rinse the cloth.

"I know you've got to be hungry," Aunt Selma said to Jesse. "Have some soup."

Jesse looked at Aunt Selma with uncertainty, then over at Uncle Mike as he sat back down.

"Go ahead, little man," Uncle Mike said, patting him on the head. "Gotta get you strong again."

Jesse spooned some of the broth out of the bowl, blew on it softly, and sipped. He spooned out more, blew, sipped. After a few more sips, he put the spoon down, lifted the bowl to his lips, and slurped hungrily. A few minutes later the bowl was empty.

"You want some more?" Aunt Selma asked.

Jesse nodded. Aunt Selma nodded at Uncle Mike, who grabbed the bowl and ladled more out at the stove. Laying the bowl back down in front of Jesse, he all of a sudden jerked his head up, then bent slightly, placing his hands on his knees and wheezing. He covered his mouth and erupted in a fit of coughing. His body shook and his face turned red. Still wheezing as the fit came to an end, he grabbed his chair and sat back down.

"Believe it or not, I'm feeling better," he said.

---

Wilmer strode to his car, parked on the street outside Emergency Hospital No. 8. The sun was beginning to set on another day, and he was going to allow himself to spend the night at home. He was also going to allow himself to kiss his wife. He would then get undressed, take a long bath, and eat a full meal before collapsing onto the bed. He would soak in as much sleep as possible before facing another day.

But tomorrow would be different. There was no way it couldn't be. Because today had been different from yesterday.

Wilmer knew now that Philadelphia's fever had broken. He'd spent all day visiting hospitals citywide to see exactly what the conditions were in each. Yes, there had been many deaths at all of them. But the fact remained: in every hospital there were fewer new cases today than yesterday. The trend was reversing.

Yes, tomorrow would be different.

Wilmer got into his car and pulled out onto South Broad Street, passing some of the street-cleaning crews the mayor had sent out. The streets were largely deserted. Folks were still holed up in their homes. But soon, he knew, they would venture out. To speak to neighbors, to see if any stores were open, or just to sit on their front stoops and enjoy being outside. Maybe not today, maybe not tomorrow. But the worst was over, and one day soon the city would come back to life.

Every few blocks Wilmer passed a wagon or truck laden with bodies. But even there he saw a hopeful sign: there were fewer bodies in them. A few days ago bodies would have been piled high in the back of every wagon on every block. Not today, Wilmer thought. And not tomorrow.

Twenty minutes later Wilmer pulled onto his street and parked his car in front of his apartment in North Philadelphia. Within moments his wife had opened the front door and was standing on the stoop with a towel pressed against her nose and mouth. Wilmer sighed with exhaustion, grabbed his briefcase, and walked slowly to the door. On the porch he reached his hand up to his wife's face, gently grabbed the towel, and pulled it away from her mouth. He leaned in for a kiss.

———

At St. Charles, Sister Katherine, dressed in her hospital clothes, knelt at the altar in the chapel nave and crossed herself. The chapel was empty. She thought everyone must be either at the cemetery or scattered at hospitals throughout Philadelphia. It was early evening, though the sun had not set. She had just bowed her head to pray when she heard the chapel door open with a creak. Turning her head, she saw Tim step inside, still dressed in his muddy overalls. They nodded at each other.

Tim padded down the aisle and knelt next to Sister Katherine, who now had her head bowed again and her eyes closed. He looked up at the figure of Christ on the cross above them. Shaking his head slowly, his lips trembling, he whispered, "Why?"

Sister Katherine gazed over at Tim. His eyes, now filled with tears, met hers.

"Why, Sister?"

Sister Katherine knew there was no answer she could give. What answer could explain so much death, so much loss, so much horror and anguish? She herself was tired of the only answer she'd been able to think of: "We can't know God's plan."

So she said nothing. She placed her hand on Tim's back to comfort him as he lowered his head to her shoulder, sobbing.

———⋅◦⋅◦⋅———

Thomas stepped into the gymnasium at Elwyn and looked around for Isaac's bed. There he was, his tiny head on the pillow. Thomas noticed that, a few rows over, Georgie's bed was empty.

Thomas padded over quietly. He stood over Isaac, and the face on the pillow did not look good. Isaac's tongue was sticking out slightly and off to the side of his mouth. Worse, he didn't appear to be breathing. There was no wheezing, no coughing. Not even a rising and falling of the chest.

"Isaac?" Thomas whispered. He knelt down and brought his face closer. "Isaac? It's Thomas, from St. Charles."

Isaac didn't answer. Thomas's heart sank.

"Isaac," Thomas said, grabbing his tiny hand. But to his surprise, the hand was not cold.

"Looking for me?" Isaac said, opening his bulging eyes and smiling.

"Isaac! You're okay!"

"Yessir, doing much better, all things considered," Isaac said in his hoarse little-boy voice. "Except I can't find my legs. Have you seen them anywhere?"

"And Georgie?"

Isaac looked over at the empty bed.

"I'm afraid our Georgie was sicker than we thought." He quickly wiped a tear from his eye.

"I'm so sorry, Isaac," Thomas said. "I truly am. But at least now he is in heaven. From what I know of him, he's probably having a ball."

He pulled a chair over and sat down next to Isaac. "Is there anything I can get you?"

"Of course there is," Isaac said. "But I doubt that you've brought any whiskey with you, seeing as you're a good Christian boy."

Thomas smiled sheepishly.

"So," Isaac said, "I'll have to settle for a cup of water."

Thomas went to the nurses' station and came back with a cup that he placed in Isaac's tiny hand. He then pulled something out of his satchel and sat down.

"You in the mood for a little Dickens?" he asked. Isaac looked over and saw that Thomas was holding a dog-eared copy of *Great Expectations*. "I picked up my old copy from school."

Isaac smiled and laid his head back onto his pillow. He coughed and cleared his throat theatrically, then stretched out his hand to give Thomas the floor.

"By all means, Sir Thomas. One can always count on a Dickens novel to make one feel better about one's own life, don't you think?"

Thomas nodded.

"And hell," Isaac continued, "it'll at least keep you from asking any more dull questions."

---

Harriet stopped in the middle of South Street, bent down, and picked up a penny she saw glimmering in the fading sunlight.

"Find a penny, pick it up, all day long you'll have good luck," she said softly to herself.

"Well," Barium said, "it's about time we had a little good luck, huh?"

"Yeah, but for longer than a day."

They continued making their way down South Street in silence. As they walked, a few wagons rolled past them, carrying bodies.

"There's not so many people in that one," Harriet said.

"Yeah. Maybe folks are starting to get better."

Harriet's face fell, and she sucked in a breath of air as she experienced a pang of grief. She'd lost everything. Everyone. Where were they all now? She could still see the ribbon in her mother's hair waving in the breeze.

They arrived at the apartment building. Aunt Selma and Uncle Mike's apartment. It was their apartment now, too. Their new home. At least for a little while. Barium opened the front door to the building and held it open for Harriet, who stepped up into the hallway and headed up the stairs to the apartment. Then Barium followed after her.

Harriet put her hand on the doorknob, then hesitated. She and Barium looked at each other for a few long seconds before she turned the knob.

Inside, Aunt Selma, Uncle Mike, and Jesse were sitting at the kitchenette table. Jesse had a bowl raised to his lips and was slurping and grunting as he eagerly swallowed. Aunt Selma looked at Harriet and Barium with tired eyes as the door opened. Waving them in, she stood up to get their soup ready.

# Epilogue

*It will not be soon forgotten how, toiling far into
the night, you dug graves, and after saying the prayers for
the dead you carried decomposing corpses in your arms,
and then buried them with your own hands.*

—Archbishop of Philadelphia Dennis J. Dougherty,
in a letter of thanks to the seminarians

THE FEROCITY AND HORROR OF the influenza attack upon
Philadelphia in October did not extend into November. By
October 20, in fact, the daily death rate dropped and there were
fewer and fewer new cases reported. But the infection rate in
Philadelphia during the epidemic was the most explosive in the
country. Among major US cities, Philadelphia recorded the third-
worst death rate, behind the Pennsylvania cities of Scranton and
Pittsburgh. South Philadelphia, where the fictional characters
of Harriet, Harry, and Barium resided in tenement housing, was
the most thoroughly infected neighborhood in the city.

On November 20, 1918, Wilmer Krusen recorded that
there had been 12,687 flu-related deaths in Philadelphia from
"when [the flu] first manifested itself, until it began to subside
Nov. 8." Krusen's numbers ended up being on the low end—esti-
mates from later studies would go as high as 19,000 dead.

At Holy Cross Cemetery the highest number of burial
permits issued for one day was 269, on October 14. The
first week of November saw a sharp decline in the number

of bodies buried—161. The seminarians (fictionalized here as Tim, Thomas, Leo, and Richard) continued their work at Holy Cross until November 5, at which time they returned to their studies. During October they buried 3,447 bodies. From November until February grave workers transferred the dead from the great trench into proper grave plots. The superintendent at Holy Cross during the transferal found that there was no single instance of the location of a body being improperly recorded or its identification confused—a testament to the careful work done by the seminary students in charge of registration of the dead.

Mayor Smith left office in 1920 but remained active in various social lodges such as the Masons. He was never punished for any of his crimes, which included complicity in the killing of a Philadelphia police officer during election violence that he helped orchestrate. When asked in the 1920s about the officer's death, he was reported to have scoffed and laughed. He died in 1949.

After the epidemic Wilmer Krusen continued to serve as a highly respected member of the city board of health. In the late 1920s he was appointed head of the new Philadelphia Department of Health and was lauded for assisting Blockley Hospital with a massive building program. He died in 1932.

The influenza epidemic of 1918 extended far beyond Philadelphia and even the United States. An estimated one-third of the world's population became infected during the three waves of the epidemic, and as many as fifty million people died. At the time the virus was known as the Spanish flu, which gives the wrong impression that it originated in Spain. It actually developed that name because Spain was neutral during

World War I, which meant that the Spanish government didn't censor the press the way British, French, and German governments did (they didn't want any stories published that would hurt national morale). Therefore, Spanish newspapers were free to report on the disease that was rearing its head, tracing its spread domestically—eight million in Spain became sick, including the king—and as it emerged in other countries. In the popular imagination, therefore, reports of the flu were tied to Spain, and the nickname stuck.

Although it is not known with certainty where exactly the virus began, one popular theory holds that it emerged in winter 1918 in an army camp in Kansas, came east as American troops mobilized for war, then exploded in Europe before returning to America on ships full of infected soldiers.

The first wave lasted from around March until midsummer, cutting a swath through Portugal, Greece, England, Scotland, Wales, Germany, Denmark, Norway, Holland, India, China, New Zealand, Australia, Algeria, Tunisia, and Egypt, among other countries. But in this initial wave of the epidemic, the number of deaths was small relative to the number who would fall ill during the ferocious and highly fatal second wave, which hit from September to November. October, the month during which most of the action in *People of the Plague* takes place, was the deadliest month. A third, milder wave occurred in many nations in early 1919.

One of the most shocking attributes of the epidemic of 1918 was that so many of its victims were young and healthy. Death from flu tends to be associated with the elderly, but in 1918 the opposite was true. Influenza death rates for people between fifteen and thirty-four years of age were twenty times higher than in previous years. Overall, nearly half of the influenza-related deaths in 1918 were of adults between twenty and forty years of age, a phenomenon unique to that epidemic.

Many questions remain unanswered about the origins of the disease, its unusual features, and its virulence. We do finally know what the virus looks like, thanks to samples of it taken from the body of a victim frozen in permafrost in Alaska, as well as samples of lung tissue preserved in the United States and Britain. Research continues, but scientists still don't have conclusive proof of how the virus developed. We do know that it started in birds, and some theories hold that the virus jumped quickly—almost immediately—from birds to humans, while other characteristics of the virus suggest it transferred to other mammals very briefly before entering the human population.

Scientists and public health officials fear that a similar strain of the virus could very well emerge in the future.

# Author's Note

WRITING AND RESEARCHING A HISTORICAL novel about the influenza epidemic of 1918 presented an interesting challenge. There were, of course, many flu victims in many parts of the country, but thorough records left by survivors of the plague proved impossible to find. Many short anecdotes have been published in various books, but I could find no complete diaries or journals, no family histories, no detailed accounting of a person's or a family's day-to-day experience. Comprehensive stories of survival have largely been lost among the death and chaos of the epidemic.

Instead, I created composites—fictionalized characters based upon real-life survivors such as Susanna Turner, Harriet Ferrell, Selma Epp, Anna Milani, Mary Volz, and William Maxwell. I encountered these survivors in books such as John Barry's *The Great Influenza* and Alfred Crosby's *America's Forgotten Pandemic,* as well as in the PBS documentary *Influenza 1918.* I infused these characters with details from the above-mentioned sources so that the story I told was as true-to-life as possible. I chose to set the story in Philadelphia because its experience of the epidemic was unusual in that it spread so rapidly among the population. South Philadelphia's overcrowded tenements were hit particularly hard by the epidemic, so I created the tenement-dwelling characters of Harriet, Harry, and Barium.

The seminary students are also fictionalized versions of real people. The plotline involving Timothy Buckley, Thomas Ryan, and Leo Naylor was inspired by Reverend Thomas C.

Brennan's book, *Records of the American Catholic Historical Society of Philadelphia,* Volume XXX. Records of the Catholic Church's work during the epidemic also included many accounts of nuns helping the sick in homes and in emergency hospitals throughout Philadelphia. I used these stories to create the fictionalized character of Sister Katherine, too.

On the other hand, both Wilmer Krusen and Mayor Smith were real people. James Higgins, author of *Keystone of an Epidemic,* served as an advisor on this novel, and he helped ensure that Krusen and Smith were accurately realized. Higgins, whose book focuses specifically on the influenza's impact on the state of Pennsylvania and whose help with this manuscript has been heroic, takes a much more sympathetic view than John Barry does of Krusen's role in the fight against the plague. Barry is extremely critical of Krusen's lack of action, casting him as a weak spectator of the epidemic rather than as a well-intentioned public health official overwhelmed by circumstance. Higgins's presentation of Krusen as powerless in the face of a public health calamity is compelling and, to my mind, more nuanced than the one-dimensional bad guy painted by Barry.

My overall goal with *People of the Plague* was to do justice to this terrifying event in our history, one that impacted the entire world and yet has been largely forgotten. It was also important for me to offer unblinking glimpses of the grotesque, including the way that this virus killed its victims, while not allowing that imagery to overshadow the stories at the heart of the novel—a constant balancing act, as there was no shortage of grim details to include! Finally, I wanted to present a realistic picture of the fear and terror that so many people must have endured when the disease reared its merciless head. It's my hope that *People of the Plague* honors the lives of both those who were taken by the influenza as well as survivors like William Maxwell, who was just ten years old when he became ill with the flu and his mother died. He said years later that, after his mother's death, "there was a sadness which had not existed before, a deep-down sadness that never went away because I knew that people weren't safe and nobody's safe. Terrible things could happen, to anybody."

# Photo Credits

COVER
Courtesy of the US Naval History and Heritage Command

CHAPTER 1
Page 2: Courtesy of the Library of Congress
Page 7: Courtesy of the National Archives and Records Administration
Page 11: Courtesy of Temple University Libraries
Page 15: Courtesy of the US Naval History and Heritage Command

CHAPTER 2
Page 19: Courtesy of the National Archives and Records Administration
Page 25: Courtesy of the US Naval History and Heritage Command

CHAPTER 3
Page 33: Courtesy of the National Archives and Records Administration
Page 38: Courtesy of Temple University Libraries
Page 41: Courtesy of the US Naval History and Heritage Command

CHAPTER 4
Page 50: Courtesy of the US Naval History and Heritage Command

CHAPTER 5
Page 54: Courtesy of the Philadelphia Archdiocesan Historical Research Center

CHAPTER 6
Page 65: Courtesy of the Library of Congress

CHAPTER 7
Page 78: Courtesy of the Philadelphia Archdiocesan Historical Research Center
Page 83: Courtesy of the National Archives and Records Administration
Page 88: Courtesy of the Philadelphia Archdiocesan Historical Research Center

CHAPTER 8
Page 100: Courtesy of Temple University Libraries
Page 104: Courtesy of the Institute of the History of Medicine

CHAPTER 9
Pages 116–117: Courtesy of the Institute of the History of Medicine

CHAPTER 10
Page 130: Courtesy of the Philadelphia Archdiocesan Historical Research Center

ALSO IN THE
HORRORS OF HISTORY
SERIES

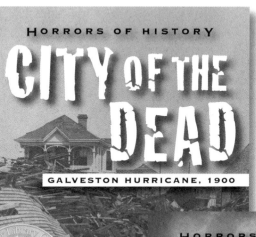

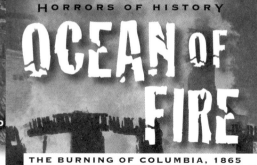